I'll Ruin Everything You Are:
Ending Western Propaganda on Red China

RAMIN MAZAHERI

Badak Merah Semesta
2019

I'll Ruin Everything You Are: Ending Western Propaganda on Red China

Cover Photos by: John Torcasio (cc-by-sa-4.0)
Cover Design by: Rossie Indira
Layout by: Rossie Indira

First edition, 2019

Published by PT. Badak Merah Semesta
Jl. Madrasah Azziyadah 16, Jakarta
http://badak-merah.weebly.com
email: badak.merah.press@gmail.com

ISBN: 978-602-50954-3-6

My little China girl
You shouldn't mess with me
I'll ruin everything you are

...

And when I get excited
My little China girl says,
"Oh baby, just you shut your mouth."
She says, "Shhhhhhh...."

~ David Bowie - *China Girl* (1983)

Ramin Mazaheri

Dedication

Dedicated to China's success in building a "moderately prosperous society" for all.

And to the Chinese members of my family.

And to my cousin who loves Chinese BBQ.

Ramin Mazaheri

Special Thanks

Special thanks to two websites: The Saker and The Greanville Post.

These articles first appeared in a serialised form on those two admirable websites, and without their help and support this book would not have been made. I extend my sincere thanks to all of their staff.

www.thesaker.is

www.greanvillepost.com

Ramin Mazaheri

By the same author

Socialism's Ignored Success Story:
Iranian Islamic Socialism

Ramin Mazaheri

Content

Ramin Mazaheri

Foreword

*E*ver since the United States became the world's main superpower at the end of World War II, they began to behave like they knew everything about the world, and that only they could provide solutions to its problems. Unfortunately, their arrogance has cost themselves and our world very dearly.

I have lived in the US for thirty years. When people ask me if I "know" the US, I still tell people that I actually do not know America that well. I know my students in the classroom, but I do not know how they interact with their parents when they go home. I know my colleagues and professors at work, but I do not know how they interact with their children and wives or husband at home. Therefore, my knowledge about America is very limited and incomplete. But some American scholars who came to China just a few times or visited other places briefly apparently feel that they "know" China and other places better than most of the natives.

Of course, America's ruling elite never want the people in the US to know what is really going on in China. They only want the American people to know *what they want them to know* about what is going on in China. If American people knew that there is an alternative way of life in the world, the American ruling class will have a difficult time to continue their business as usual. This is the reason behind their many "Cold Wars" around the world. Much American scholarship about China and the rest of the world was purposely distorted because the rich American foundations, which finance American scholarship, wanted it to be that way. Some scholars, in order to get financial support from these powerful foundations, had to twist their findings to please their funding sources. The irony is that they are deceiving themselves by creating such misinformation about China and the rest of the world. In the end, the chickens will come home to roost.

The Chinese Communist Party did not try to please everybody in China. The Chinese Communist Party in the early days unequivocally stated that it represented the interests of the working class, and that it would suppress the interests of the capitalists. Mr. Ramin Mazaheri justly raises the question of the "1 percent versus the 99 percent" because we all live in class societies, and a world of nation states. Therefore, we should realize that there simply is no political policy, which will benefit everybody or every class equally. The Chinese Communist Party never hid its position about this.

What the Chinese Communist Government did - through land reform policies, the policies of the Great Leap Forward, the Cultural Revolution, and other programs - was to raise the socioeconomic status of the Chinese working class people, who account for over 90 percent of the Chinese population. When 90 percent of the people in a country benefit from the government's policies, that country is doing the right thing. When 90 of percent of the people in a country are uplifted, that country is uplifted.

In this book Mr. Mazaheri accurately and rightfully denigrates the work of John King Fairbank, one of America's most influential scholars on China, but we must remember that Fairbank is far from alone. In 2015 the US government's leading China expert, Michael Pillsbury, published *The One Hundred Year Marathon: China's Secret Strategy to Replace America as Global Superpower,* which became a best-selling book in its field. What a historic irony! According to Pillsbury, China has been working on this "secret strategy" since 1949 - the year America's elite dismissed the Chinese Communist government by saying that the Chinese would never be able to feed themselves, and that it would have to come back begging for America's help. Nor should we forget another example of so-called "scholarship" on China - the blockbuster book *Mao's Great Famine,* by Frank Dikotter. In the book he claimed that over forty million Chinese people starved to death during the Great Leap Forward...

and yet scandal ensued when it was found that such a lack of proof caused him to use a 1947 *Life* magazine photo to represent his claims of such starvation on the book's very cover! Dikotter also claimed that he had documents which proved that Mao wanted to starve half of the Chinese people to death during the Great Leap Forward so that the remaining half would be able to have more - it was discovered that Dikotter had misread the document, and that the opposite was true. Far more benignly, what Mao meant was to kill half of certain investment projects so that the remaining half of the projects would be completed in time. That a scholar can get away with this kind of dishonesty and fabrication in the US...whose fault is that?

In English-language literature, it is hard to find anything positive about what the Chinese government did. It reaches a point where I have to tell my students sometimes, with a bit of sarcasm, that: "It is China - how can we expect the Chinese government to do anything right?"

Now, with China's rise, there is this nonsense about China's "secret strategy" to replace the US as the premier global superpower... but there is no secret strategy on China's part. When you choose to deceive yourself, by encouraging bad scholarship on China, when you allow the dishonest scholars to get away with lies and fabrications, who do you blame? When the CIA, the best-financed intelligence service in the world, produces reports on China, which turn out to be false time after time, who do you blame?

The Chinese government and the Chinese people have no desire to challenge the United States of America. They send their children to study in the US and they buy houses in the US. They have been working very hard and have concentrated on solving their own problems. They did not meddle inside other countries. They did not fight any wars unless wars came to them. Yet FBI director Chris Wray recently claimed that China is the "most significant" threat to the United States. I want to ask him: "Why?" China became a threat simply because China has done a better job than the United States in the last 70 years. The many US officials who have made similar statements should stop blaming China for their own problems - they can only blame their own stupidity.

It is time that the public in the US and the West wake up to modern reality. I recommend Mr. Mazaheri's book to readers in China and the rest of the world because it is a refreshingly new perspective, and one which we urgently need right now. At this critical moment of our world, we need critical views like Mr. Ramin Mazaheri's.

~ Dongping Han

(Author of *The Unknown Cultural Revolution: Life and Change in a Chinese Village.* Han was raised in rural Shandong province, China, and teaches history and political science at Warren Wilson College in North Carolina.)

Ramin Mazaheri

1
Old vs. new scholarship on the continent of China

Europe is a continent and China is not only because the winners write the history books.

There is no scientific reason Europe is a continent: Europe is not a separate landmass, nor does it even sit on its own tectonic plate – we may as well call Canada a continent. China's land mass area is nearly identical with Europe's. What makes West Eurasia more special than East Eurasia?

Anyway, China is far more than just a country – it's better to think of it like the

"Islamic World", which is certainly far more than just a mass of "Arabs". "Chinese" is really a signifier of a common culture which transcends ethnicity, language, geography, an individual nation, an individual church, etc.

It's absurd to think of China as homogenous: China has nearly 60 officially recognised minorities today, and that's after a couple millennia of consolidation. There are about 100 Indo-European languages (if we rightly exclude the Indo-Iranian branch – neither of which are in Europe), but hundreds of Sinitic languages still exist (and that's even after excluding the Tibetan, South and Southeast Asian branches).

No Western dynasty or power could compare with the combined size, scope and duration of its Chinese counterparts. In the US they say, "Everything is bigger in Texas" – visit China and you'll agree they should be saying: "Everything is 10 times smaller in Texas than in China". Stand before the terracotta warriors at Xi'an and you'll see what I mean.

Is it because Europe's geography

made it as isolated as a Greek island, and thus culturally unique? China has been far more isolated than Europe: it wasn't accessible for sea trade until later in its history; most Chinese lived in only the northern plains until 1000AD; the Gobi, Hindu Kush and Himalayas all provided a huge geographic barrier; there wasn't sustained, firmly-intellectual contact with non-Chinese until the 7th century. (A good explanation of this is the book *2030*, by superb reporter Pepe Escobar. He includes fascinating and little-known historical information about Xuanzang, who served the same "East-West" uniter role that Escobar does today, thankfully.)

Personally, I think that Europe as an idea is bogus: the divide is really between Mediterranean and non-Mediterranean (Northern European) cultures -that was certainly Europe's own view for many, many centuries.

So who is arrogant, who is defensive, who is right? Let's have some fun with generalisations!

The arrogance of the West is that they believe they have the best system.

The arrogance of the Chinese is that

they believe they are the best people.

(The arrogance of Iranians is that they believe they are the best martyrs, when they are really just the best at believing that everyone else is the worst martyr!)

I would say the Chinese are closer to winning this dubious competition, because there's absolutely no doubt that the West European system (bourgeois capitalism) is not the best – in 2018 even Westerners are revolting in White Trash Revolutions across the European Union bloc and the United States. (White Trash Revolutions is a favourite class-based phrase of mine which reclaims an insult. It is similar to what Iranian's called the "Revolution of the Barefooted" in 1979.)

The Chinese have always had an apparent disinterest in the rest of the world, and that seems to imply an arrogant self-glorification. But they have some grounds for their belief: Their millennia-old meritocracy – the Civil Service Examination – made public service the highest good, was theoretically open to all, but tapped only a few.

It's a bit intimidating to think that one

must compete with 1500 years of cumulative efforts of their best and brightest, no? Also, their neo-Confucian hierarchy of "gentry/scholar, farmer, craftsmen / tradesman, merchant", with soldiers held in such low esteem that they don't even make the official list, is such a high-minded inverse of the Western view that one surely does a double-take when learning about it for the first time. Thankfully, China shows that such a social system is actually feasible.

And it's especially hard to counter the arrogance of China in 2018, as they are the world's most successful socialist country ever, and also the most successful country today in a host of key areas.

Perhaps it is because I hail from a humble, small, self-denying people who only live to serve God and his children with good works (I'm such a good martyr!) that I have no sour grapes for China's apparent victory over the West. Anyway, since 1979 Iran's motto has been "Neither East nor West" so I'm rather above such low-minded competition (bad martyr – so arrogant!).

White Trash conundrum: Where do humble people learn when no learning is available?

The problem is: Since 1949 it has been virtually impossible to find any English-language studies of China, which did not primarily exist to elevate the West over China. All the West has – or wants – when it comes to China analysts is either an alarmist or a denier.

So from academia to journalism, prior to the internet – one had very little chance to find honest reporting on China or from China. Pro-Chinese viewers were *verboten*. This obvious lack of objectivity means that the average Westerner seemingly knows nothing of Chinese history other then the idea of an imperial emperor and a farmer in a huge bamboo hat... and China is a continent!

Ignorance is dangerous: Even if the West wanted to defeat China – and Obama's (failed) "Pivot to China" shows that they do – they could not, because they do not even know their enemy. Such ignorance has already led them to catastrophic bloodletting in Indochina and

Korea, Afghanistan & Iraq, and many other places besides.

The alternative to scholarship which exists to elevate the West over China is a scholarship which sympathetically tries to understand China on its own terms and merits. And isn't that a humble starting point? Thankfully for those who want to learn about China, in 2018 we finally have this option, largely thanks to the internet. There is a new scholarship on China which the West just can't suppress anymore.

Remember the bad old days?

Many years ago I asked a professor-friend in academia who taught Chinese history for a top comprehensive history on that little hamlet. He suggested, *China: A New History* by John King Fairbank (First published in 1992, second edition in 2006).

I can see why this is the English-speaking world's most popular university-level textbook on China – it ticks all the establishment boxes: Fairbank was educated at Exeter and Oxford, became Harvard's first-ever China scholar, was known as "the West's doyen on China", and this book was his "masterwork" which killed him – he died of a heart attack the day he submitted it to his publisher.

My sincere condolences. While it may be fine on the bone oracles of the Shang Dynasty, it is rather pure junk when it comes to dealing with modern China. But I figured that going in: I did not expect anything but a rabid fear of Red China, the casual arrogance that the Western model is superior and a total glossing over of both Communist China's successes & the West's crimes in China.

I wanted the academic viewpoint because I didn't expect much from Western journalists, who I know already genuflect at the altar of the Fairbank-types (dead or alive). If you do look to journalists, the only comprehensive history on China which is ranked more popular (just slightly) on Amazon than Fairbank's academic work is John Keay's *China: A History*. Keay is a longtime reporter for *The Economist*, which is as editorially-sympathetic to Red China as is the CIA (or as is Harvard's establishment).

Clearly, selecting Fairbank as a "standard bearer" for Western scholarship on China is a fair and appropriate for a book such as this one.

On the other side, open-minded readers finally have new, better, accurate resources, which are best exemplified by Jeff J. Brown's truly indispensable *China is Communist, Dammit!* (2017).

Brown comes from two fundamentally different places than Fairbank: the outside and the inside.

Brown is not trying to join the establishment, apparently feels no responsibility to unquestioningly uphold it, and thus has all the editorial control of an outsider; Brown is also living inside China, and it seems fair to assume that he has to actually be sympathetic and understanding of those around him, in order to avoid repeated bouts of culture shock and homesickness.

People will say that Brown's title shows his bias...and I see nothing wrong with that accusation or the title itself. "Objective journalism" is equal parts goal and myth: "One person's 'freedom fighter' is another person's 'terrorist'", and I learned that on the very first day of journalism school.

I actually object to Fairbank's title far

more. It should have been: *China: A Rewritten History*, because it certainly is not the history the Chinese know and believe – *it's the Chinese history the West wants to believe.* And that is unfortunate for Fairbanks and his readers... but it is also exactly why Fairbanks gets the laurels while Brown is probably hoping just a few people actually buy his book, dammit!

(Is Brown secretly 1/8th Iranian or something? What a martyr! Sell out already, sheesh!)

The beauty of Brown's book is that it helps provide a balance which anyone interested in China has long been lacking and desiring. It is truly a one-of-a-kind book, and I would not be surprised if, over the decades, it gets translated widely because it is so very necessary. In short: the book contains truly excellent analysis, but it's especially unique because of the sheer number of monumental facts and in-depth anecdotes which non-Chinese refuse to admit or discuss – where else can they be found but in this book?

Brown does not work for *The Economist*, so the mainstream media is never going to review his book, but I was happy to do so in this journalism series. I'm certain that Brown will go down as one of the "first movers" in the development of a new trend: Western analysts who gave up on attacking China.

Think of all we've been missing by misunderstanding China

Even before reading either Brown's book or this one, I think one must concede: Year after year and decade after decade, the West has underestimated the vibrancy, stability and success of the Chinese model. It is therefore fair to conclude that their analysis is fundamentally flawed in some way.

The aim of this book is two-fold: Firstly, it will compare how Fairbank and Brown, two very different authors, analysed the three primary events of modern China – the Great Leap Forward, the Cultural Revolution & the legacy of Mao. Secondly, it will synthesise the very different groups of facts, anecdotes and analyses presented by these two authors in order to arrive at: modern analytical conclusions about China, possible parallels of the Chinese experience with other countries, and also continue with the ongoing modern debate of socialism versus capitalism.

By contrasting the old and new scholarship on China one can see which is accurate and which is not, and why. By unlearning unsympathetic & un-objective scholarship on China and learning sympathetic scholarship on China from one rooted in China for some 20 years, we can confidently move forward towards greater global understanding.

China is daunting – after all, how can the West understand a China which has been culturally anti-capitalist since '49...BC, that is? True, modern, unbiased understanding of any continent is a major task, but quite an edifying one.

The bottom line is that the Western establishment's view is so ideologically-driven, so unsympathetic, so willfully opposed to accepting the native's view of themselves, that it can fairly be called "extremist". (An irony is that some will view this statement as unfair, yet will label Brown's work "extremist" without hesitation....)

Ultimately, extremism is a tactic used to confuse the issue and to deliberately reduce understanding...and that's what this book tries to subvert. Holding up old and new scholarship, combined with a younger viewpoint, can provide the reader with some interesting insights thanks to cross-pollination.

The true credit goes to the modern scholarship of those like Brown's, which does something which 20th century scholars did not want to do: clarify the impressive humanity of 21st century China.

Rest assured that China knows all about the last 500 years of Western history, which it experienced first-hand during their 110 years (1839-1949) of Western & Japanese control (many include Japan with the West, quite fairly) which they remember as the "century of humiliation". That's a pretty harsh assessment of themselves for the Chinese to carry around, no? Such honesty redounds to their credit.

The reality is that the West has only themselves to blame for their huge "mutual knowledge gap" in 2018 - it is due to their vast anti-Communist China campaign.

Thankfully, today we can finally access authors like Brown, who have compiled superb, comprehensive scholarship to allow today's readers to grant China the seriousness and honesty it deserves. The Fairbanks of the Western world remain firmly in place - providing employment at university presses and rubber-stamping overpriced diplomas. Daily hack journalists such as myself - I am Iran-based PressTV's correspondent in Paris - have something small but rather crucial to offer: the importance and urgency of the moment, which we hacks are reminded of with every story's deadline.

Whether or not we choose to apply modern China's solutions to our native problems is another question, and up to the reader, but willfully ignoring their solutions is so prejudiced that it cannot honestly be called "scholarship", nor "intelligent", "tolerant" or "enlightened".

The first step to achieving those worthy adjectives is to re-examine Chinese history during their communist era. Due to

China's success and the West's decline in 2018, one should not blindly accept the Western interpretation of Chinese history during the modern socialist era.

2

Daring to go beyond Western propaganda on the Great Leap Forward's famine

Between 108 BC and 1911 AD there were no fewer than 1,828 recorded famines in China, or nearly one each year.

Therefore, since 1962 there should have been in China – if their historical average remained unchanged – 50 serious famines. Instead there have been zero.

When one discusses the Great Leap Forward's famine, how often do you hear this point of view rooted in the reality of Chinese history?

I wonder: Given 50+ years of success, how much longer can the West wave this bloody shirt? Will there still be a thriving Great Leap famine intellectual cottage industry in 50 years? 100 years? 200 years...?

Kudos to you if you are a reasonable person who prefers fairness and honesty to anti-socialist animosity of the knee-jerk variety, but even that one fact doesn't allow us to fully appreciate how difficult it was for the Chinese Communist Party to have defeated famine since the Great Leap Forward.

We can blame Mother Nature: Topographically, China is very far from India. Wide-open India can allow cows to graze in peace, but mountainous China can only afford to allot just 2% of its land for pasture, compared with 50% for the US. Nearly 90% of China's farmland has to go for crops because they have to feed 20% of the world's population, and from just 6% of the world's arable land. Around 85% of the population already lives on the one-third of land which is arable, and there is little chance that they can increase this amount of arable land. The South farms year round, but in Northern China, where "China" began, the topography and climate is akin to the Midwestern United States or Ukraine; however, average annual rainfall is a US Dust Bowl-like 25 inches, with annual variances of 30%, making the region especially prone to famine.

No wonder Chinese farmers backed the central planning, cooperation and easy credit of socialism....capitalistic individualism could obviously never thrive in such harsh conditions. This cultural fact well-predates 1949 whether one likes it or not: the jǐng, or well-field, system which began all the way back in the 9th century BC is fairly considered a sort of early socialism. Picture a tic-tac-toe board, with its 9 equal parts (or the # sign); in the centre square was the well, and that area was communally farmed to pay taxes to the aristocracy and emperor; the other 8 parts were farmed individually. Quite a lot of individual capitalism, perhaps, but clearly some socialism and a lot of egalitarian distribution of land.

China's famines were constant (are we not grateful that we can switch to the past tense now?) despite a 2 millennia-old system of centralised imperialism so cooperative and well-planned that ancient farmers knew they were growing crops expressly to be shipped to a famine-prone region on the other side of China. Such central planning is what allows unity, China will attest. This view is the polar opposite of today's Germans, who turn their immoral noses up at the idea of showing solidarity with debt-blighted Greeks (who were blighted by German bankers, of course).

China's governments – imperialist and communist – are clearly notable for their efforts to limit the anti-harmony societal disorder caused by unrestrained individualism. Indeed Mao's food procurement policies – taking food from those who grew it and giving it to the less successful farmers – was truly a continuation of age-old cultural policy; it is only the West that derides this policy as a horrible violation of their supreme sanctity, which is: "my private property is all mine".

And despite all of these constraints and historical proofs of guaranteed failures, in 2018 China's malnutrition is lower than in developed countries. China exports food! Accordingly, in 2016 the UN's World Food Program signed a memorandum of understanding intended to help developing countries learn from China's success in fighting hunger.

Hunger should be treated in the same way as a natural disaster; Iran's biggest curse is earthquakes and, were it not for vast anti-Iran sentiment, many more would learn about our similarly amazing, socialist-inspired techniques for dealing with the aftermaths of earthquakes.

The Chinese Communist Party has seemingly done the impossible – ended the scourge of famine in China.

Yet, despite all this success, the famine of the Great Leap Forward is the single-most important pillar in the West's anti-China propaganda. It is all the proof one Westerner must cite in order to discredit the Communist Party, Mao and any of China's socioeconomic successes.

Such a view is clearly a benefit for the 1%, or the elite, who never suffer from famine. Thankfully, we have new scholarship on Red China which focuses on the view from the starving 99%, and which cares for sustenance more than preserving the status quo and the West's claim of total ideological superiority.

The West's false 'moral causes' of the Great Leap's Famine

The 1959-61 famine is not close to China's worst famine, historically: you had three famines which claimed 15, 30 and 45 million people in the 19th century alone. Six million died in 1927, and there were major famines in 1929, 1939 and 1942. This is, sadly, a very inadequate list.

All of these were caused by environmental factors, and of course by political factors as well: it's not as if China didn't have a government back then – it's just that they didn't have a government which could cope...in undeniable contrast to China over the last 50+ years.

I am not saying that the deaths of 15-20 million people were not important – I'm accurately adding that they were, sadly, not unusual in China whatsoever. Nobody honest would consider this context of near-annual famines irrelevant, but the West focuses like a laser on the Great Leap Forward's famine in an usually-ahistorical vacuum, and that makes their view obviously quite flawed and easily rebutted.

For the West, the Great Leap's famine was caused by ineffective, overpaid bureaucrats who worked for a totalitarian regime...along with the routine implication that the Communist Party inflicted this famine *on purpose* in order to settle scores / intimidate the populace / hoard wealth for themselves / because they are inherently immoral and callous in a way which capitalists could never be, and other such similar nonsense.

Another common Western stereotype in scholarship on the Great Famine – and a routine "explanation" for Fairbank in his book – is the "*docility*" of the Chinese farmer. This "*docility*", it is implied, is the only way they would have allowed the Communist Party to take control, and the Chinese just plain lack the testosterone which the West has in spades and which is their aggressive answer to everything. I guess we need to get Chinese peasants some crystal meth to pep them up? That method sure worked before...for the West:

getting 1/4th the Chinese population to use opium smoothed the path to their "Century of Humiliation" by the West & Japan.

The histories of those 19th century famines are appalling – entire villages dead by hunger, bodies everywhere, no rain for three years, deaths coming quickly...but death by hunger must seem quite long.

The difference between academia and journalism is that journalists usually have a direct and limited point to make, for which they use a small amount of facts (due to a limited amount of space); academia is claiming to describe a totality, in which they make objective-sounding points in an indirect manner, and buttress them with a great number of facts. But even establishment Fairbank can't go as low as most journalists and say that the Great Leap's Famine was a calculated, genocidal policy:

"In 1959-60 China was better organized, and famine areas full of starved corpses were not seen. But malnutrition due to thin rations made millions more susceptible to disease. The higher-than-

usual mortality did not become known until the statistics were worked out. Not until 1960 was it finally realized that many peasants were starving...."

I will prove later how quickly the Chinese Communist Party reacted humanely after 1960 to change policy. But before any exoneration there must first be reasonable explanation.

The simple, understandable, all-too-human reasons for the famine

Socialism has to be built: After all, what the heck is an agricultural cooperative where farmers are running things? For the millennia the system was: "This is the tax – you pay now!"

But once China's gentry was kicked out and the farmers gathered round as equals...this was the question to which they could only scratch their heads, think, and start drawing up diagrams in the dirt.

Therefore, of course the Great Leap Forward was inefficient in some ways: Socialism is something, which has to be constructed, daily, still, because socialism has to make itself up as it goes along. This was certainly more true in 1960 than it is after 58 more years of socialist experience; a good example of how socialism is learning was Fidel Castro's final wish - no monuments or statues, in an obvious effort to prevent any sort of cult of personality like North Korea's Kim. But even in 2018, due to such a lack of support from the Western world, socialism remains an exciting and new social experiment - society has to experiment on itself, and often in an immensely hostile environment, both internationally and domestically (from their deposed elite class). This obviously implies an increased risk for failure, but only in the short term. It certainly contains the moral exoneration of its superior choices - the capitalist status quo was certain to be worse in the short, medium and long terms.

China realised in the late 1950s that they had to create a new method – the Soviet model could not apply to farmer-dominated China. The Great Leap Forward represents the point when the Chinese broke with the USSR because they needed

Chinese solutions to Chinese problems, not Russian solutions to Chinese problems.

It's terrible how Western propaganda can turn up into down, but: The Great Leap Forward was not caused by increased totalitarian oppression of the Communists on farmers – it was actually fuelled by not enough central control. I quote here Fairbank, because not only do you likely think I am not objective, but because you may mistakenly not realise that socialism is truly based on giving power to the average worker, not taking it away:

"*For this purpose there was a general decentralisation of economic management in 1957. Many enterprises and even monetary controls were decentralised down to the local level. The central statistical bureau was broken up and localised together with functions of economic planning. This was the context in which the overambitious targets of the Great Leap were formulated in each locality, not by economists, but by cadres inspired by emulation who were contemptuous of experts but intensely loyal to the cause.*"

(The "*experts*" here are likely

capitalists, as this is Fairbank, after all.)

And that is a Western academic assessment – it is quite the opposite of the journalistic scaremongering of power-grabbing Mao, no? In fact, we see how Mao (as he did time and again) rejected the centralisation of power in himself – this very idea is impossible for many individualistic Westerners to grasp – and how socialism is a constant devolution of power from the king to the local person.

I continue with that same passage to show how the Great Leap Forward succeeded in many ways. Of course, the average Chinese person was thrilled and electrified to finally be empowered in their own lives...yet all we hear about is the famine:

"The result in 1958 was a mighty paroxysm of round-the-clock labor. The face of the country was changed with new roads, factories, cities, dikes, dams, locks, afforestation, and cultivation, for which the 650 million Chinese had been mobilised in nationwide efforts of unparalleled intensity and magnitude."

As any modern analysis of China admits, this is the true bedrock of Chinese economic success post-1980: the Mao-era programs which literally built the infrastructure needed to allow the emergence of a middle class. Yet for the West Chinese economic success starts only *after* the death of Mao. Yet none of those dams or roads have disappeared, nor are they any less indispensable to the 21st century Chinese economy.

These points are well-known to those who care, but are obsessively blocked by the West. I will not persevere on these myriad positive economic points of the Mao era – though that would be a fair analytical tactic – thanks to new China scholarship, you can easily find them!

Back to the true causes of the famine.

OVER-ZEALOUSNESS!!! I love the smell of socialism in the morning!

Overzealousness was also seen during the first Soviet collectivisations, and it produced the exact same problems and phenomena I will describe here. Overzealousness is thus a historically-proven risk which any newly-socialist nation should expect and guard against.

It is very, easily explainable if we simply imagine Mao and the Chinese as humans, instead of monsters / "*docile*" idiots. Let's use our informed imaginations:

At the start of China's revolution – with the foreigners finally kicked out and everyone ready to pull in the same pro-China direction – revolutionary spirit is higher than high.

The cadres report to their superiors with unassailable intentions: "Yes, we will meet our target plans, and more! Long live the Revolution and long live free China!"

The bureau secretaries mark on their report: "These guys are proven winners, after all. I'm marking them down for a 100% success rate in indelible ink!"

The party leaders say: "These are great reports! Plus, we are going to give jobs to all the unemployed, and end drug use, so how can we not exceed expectations? And all that new equipment is going to revolutionise things as well! So I'm going to promise that my region is going to over-perform the quota by 10%, and that way I'll bring great honor to my people, and my career! Utopia, here we come!"

And then...reality hits.

In the case of China in 1959, bad weather hits.

And locust plagues. Locust populations likely ballooned as a sad and unintended consequence of 1958's "Four pests" anti-disease and hygiene campaign against rats, mosquitoes, flies and especially sparrows, which upset the ecological balance and eliminated a predator of locusts.

And the books – which are based on the great year of 1958, when total food production doubled nationwide – are thus totally screwed up!

And bureaucratic, statistical chaos is just as big a problem as the decreased production, because the promised 100% of X from Region A to distribute collectively turns out to be only 30% of X. In the pre-computer age, by the time the hard data arrives that the promised X from Region A can't head to Regions B, C, G and Q, a re-ordering prompted by this failure was needed weeks ago. But the higher-ups can't meet for weeks more because they are addressing the same crisis in their home regions.

Finally, the higher-ups are able to assemble and they discuss who needs what immediately. All this time the capitalists abroad and at home are laughing gleefully that the ideal of total, equal, communist distribution has to be postponed - the Party has no time for laughing but as actually trying to do something about all that grain which has started to rot on the new rails.

What I have just written is a less academic, more humanised form of what Harvard's Fairbanks described:

"By concentrating solely on Chairman Mao as the leader we would fail to convey the national mood of fervent self-sacrifice and frenetic activity that characterised the Great Leap Forward. Peasants worked around the clock to break their own work records, cadres in charge locally kept on reporting totally unrealistic production figures, and Mao's colleagues such as the economist Chen Yun and Premier Zhou Enlai found no way to stop the fever."

Firstly, when does any capitalist ever

work that hard, eh? What is the profit motive compared to the encouraging power of the moral-political creed? Indeed, there is no comparison: As Jesus said to the devil when tempted with food during his fast: "Man does not live on bread alone." I'll tell you when a capitalist works that hard - during wartime.

The above passage – again, by someone who is definitely not sympathetic whatsoever to socialism – shows that the famine was the product of ALL the Chinese people, of good intentions, of the unexpected difficulties encountered in any new venture (such as Chinese socialism), of the sad human reality that we live in an imperfect world where bad things happen to good people and of the fact that we do not dominate Mother Nature as much as we think. The idea that "it was all Mao" is obviously pathetic propaganda.

These early problems, history proves over and over, are seemingly always encountered during the initial transition to socialism, which is such a radical change in human history: China's problems are very similar to the early difficulties in the USSR, and to early

Communist Cuba's difficulties to radically change from capitalist-imperialist one-crop dominance (sugar) to diversified agriculture, etc.

In some ways, the West's ordering of Saddam Hussein to attack Iran immediately after their revolution was a boon in that it sharply focused organisational energies on one thing – the war effort. A war economy was implemented, with rations and coupons, and that is nothing if not egalitarian. Questions of privatising an economy almost totally state-owned and guided by central planning could only begin after the war, giving the Iranian state a huge head start in controlling the economy for the benefit of the Iranian People. Despite so-called "privatisation" - which was uniquely Iranian and absolutely nothing like Western privatisation - it's fair to estimate that the Iranian government controls 100% of the economy (excluding the Black Market) today. Of course Iran remains socialism's ignored success story, due to Western Islamophobia and the outdated, ineffective and anti-democratic anti-religious sentiment of many leftists worldwide. However, Iran has become China's central hub in their One Belt, One Road or New Silk Road project because China knows that Iran is guided by rock-solid revolutionaries, who have created what I call "Iranian Islamic Socialism". It's no coincidence that the only two countries with a government-sponsored Cultural Revolution (Iran's was 1980-83) have now allied themselves for decades. I encourage readers to find my article "Parallels between Iran's Basij and the Chinese Communist Party", which describes the many governmental and cultural similarities between these two Asian countries.

Iran had the difficulty of switching to socialism and fighting a war, much like the new USSR. For more fortunate socialist-inspired countries like China, however, initial chaos at the first bump on the road is the logical and expected (or should be, by now) outcome caused by drastically reordering society from capitalism to socialism. A car's lower gears have the most torque because getting started is always the hardest part – the mistake is to kneecap yourself by giving up on the revolution when it has only just begun.

It should also not be forgotten that China's hand-farming method was already extremely difficult to improve on. Do you think there's a machine that can do as careful a job as a bent-over person scrutinising every square centimetre for weeds? No machine can beat that. In the US the problem was simply putting vast tracts of land to use – improving yields from "nothing" to "something" – but not in China, where labor was not the scarce resource but arable land, as I discussed in Chapter 1. There was thus likely a significant over-estimation of the ability of modern machines to increase production.

But what definitely increased farmer efficiency were the centrally-planned and centrally-operated major infrastructure projects: vast irrigation networks, huge road building programs to improve transportation, tunnel-building for mass drainage, lake and dam building, new railroads, steel production for all these projects, etc. And this is where the Great Leap Forward's central planning undoubtedly succeeded, and why productivity did grow.

But the ancient, backbreaking Chinese model – a family meticulously farming a small plot land with the maximum amount of care – as inefficient? That's obviously false, and their huge population despite a small amount of arable land stands as millennia-old proof. To say Chinese culture is farmer-centric – in the economic, social, cultural and ethical sense – is to say that water is wet....

The Great Leap Forward will always prove the socialist genius of Mao and China's first generation of revolutionaries (...and thus the Western propaganda effort). The primary theoretical contribution of Mao was to recognise this reality and to create a "farmer-centered" socialism, breaking away from the industrial worker-dominated socialism of the USSR, Stalinism and Trotskyism, which despite the latter's claims of universality simply did not translate into the Chinese society in which Mao lived.

The historic Sino-Soviet split occurred precisely because of the Great Leap Forward's ideological differences with the then-current Soviet model, pushed by Khrushchev. Khrushchev was an outspoken critic of the Great Leap Forward, and we must remember that leftists often commit suicide on the altar of small differences - the success of China's modifications threatened Soviet ideological dominance.

But even more than ideological dominance, Khrushchev was, as Mao correctly saw, a revisionist (revising socialism until it turns back into capitalism), and a right-wing socialist whose mantle would be carried by Gorbachev...into socialism's grave and the arms of capitalist depredation, as we all know.

There is no doubt: Mao was clearly a hugely important thinker and revolutionary, while Khrushchev is remembered as a bureaucrat who denounced Stalin for political gain (severely undermining the Soviets' ability to emulate what worked: revolutionary socialism) and who was ultimately fired for incompetence.

The Great Leap Forward, and its inherent insistence on the need for specific, nationalist / locally-based solutions, was and remains a major dagger in the Trotskyist version of a universal socialist method; furthermore, Maoism simultaneously defied and yet upheld Stalinism, stripping it of the egotistical pride it bestows upon "more advanced" factory workers, but retaining its right to pursue "socialism in one country".

This is also why the Soviets made a major contribution to the absurd idea that "China is NOT communist": the intelligent refusal of Chinese Communists to follow their Soviet advisors led to the perpetual Russian accusation that Chinese communists were mere "radishes" – red only on the outside.

The Great Leap Forward clearly marked the beginning of the ideological superiority of China over the USSR; Khrushchev's ideology marked the beginning of the Soviet's lack of revolutionary commitment, their failure to adapt their ideology to cultural ideas from other areas of the world from which they could have learned or at least supported, and their eventual descent into Yeltsin-era chaos.

Focusing on famine deaths is tabloid journalism

"If it bleeds it leads", especially if your ideological enemy is bleeding....

Western propaganda implies that the Great Leap Forward's famine was somehow a boon to Mao's bloody grab for power. It takes modern English-language scholarship to debunk those lies (from Brown):

"With the challenging Great Leap Forward, 1959-1961, Mao lost a huge amount of credibility and his ability to push his platform was weakened. He even had to transfer presidency of China to Liu Shaoqi. This is not evidence of a despotic dictator."

A major political pause was instituted in order to regroup and chart a new path. The third-five year plan would not start until 1966, four years after the ending of the 2nd 5-year plan. The Chinese People clearly became aware of the failures, and public disapproval forced political punishments accordingly. It's the "People's Democratic Dictatorship", not the Mao dictatorship....

Another viewpoint which gives the

West glaucoma is: amid bad weather, locusts, overzealousness and the usual domestic and foreign reactionary sabotage which accompanies any socialist revolution, the death toll could have been 50 million, 100 million or more. The West never even considers this line of thought, but the Chinese are well aware that the government continued to distribute rations, to coordinate between differently-hit and differently-producing regions, to provide obviously revolutionary amounts of services to peasants, that education programs went on the entire time, and that these cumulative efforts by the government likely prevented worse results amid the succession of setbacks.

And the failure to pursue this line makes it impossible for Westerners to understand why, despite the famine and hardship, the Chinese *did not abandon* the Communist Party, and why a nation awash in guns did not overthrow it violently.

Indeed, if there was a protracted hoarding by Party leaders, or a wilful refusal to aid the People, it is absurd to think that a war-hardened, widely-armed populace wouldn't have decapitated the

Party. Of course, maybe you operate from the assumption that the Chinese are "*docile*" - hey, that kind of thinking can take you all the way to Harvard!

Indeed, the CCP (Chinese Communist Party) was put in power by a popular revolution with the mandate to institute great leaps forward, and to hell with the old gods of rain, harvests, locusts, whatever.

It is also never admitted that, despite the famine and hardship, the Great Leap Forward and its agricultural revolution still empowered the peasants more than ever. Famine was not unknown to these People - at least they had some say in things now. This People-centred view – this from-below view of the very real political culture of socialism – was denied by people like Fairbank for decades, but as a historian he is obliged to at least give the broad strokes (even if he always gets defensive at the end):

> "*Once they had been called into being and had found their way upwards in society through the collectivization of agriculture, this new stratum of activists in the countryside*

needed things to do and were ready to go further. The Great Leap Forward was hard to rein in because once the activists got started reorganising the villages, they tended to keep on going. 'Liberation' in effect had produced a new class who wanted to keep on liberating."

The Chinese don't put their "*Liberation*" in quotes, as their previous status included so many shackles....which may be a minor consideration to non-Chinese, but it certainly shouldn't be.

To sum up, replacing what they have told you about Great Leap Forward is a real step towards your own liberation. Why? Because Western views are based on historical nihilism, sensationalism and deliberately misleading information.

I hope I have not given the impression of any sort of whitewashing of the Great Leap Forward's famine. Obviously, that would be dangerous and wrong, and I reject any such accusations.

I do hope I have clarified the context, actions, philosophical motivations and results of the Great Leap Forward. My main hope is that this leads to de-

demonisation of the first generation of Chinese revolutionaries, by showing that the famine was not the result of demons but well-intentioned humans in pursuit of a very modest goal, but one never seen on Earth: socio-economic equality.

'Mao's famines' were feasts compared with the West's famines

A perfectly acceptable analytical tactic – yet totally abandoned among modern Western leftists – is to force the West to admit their own crimes before they can accuse others of wrongdoing. This is a part of auto-critique - save your criticism for in private, and attack, attack, attack the reactionaries in public. Unfortunately, modern leftists have forgotten this cardinal rule, and one which is absolutely fair (and one which capitalists certainly have not forgotten).

Brown – of course not Fairbank – makes very apt trans-national comparisons of famines. He begins by accepting the opposition's high estimate of deaths during the Great Leap's famine:

"So, 30 million is 4.6% of China's total population of 654 million....Ireland lost 25% of its people during the British-legislated Great Potato Famine Genocide 1845-1853...French colonialists in Vietnam, in a terrible drought, caused two million to starve to death in 1945, which was 7% of the local population. The United States massacred 7% of the Filipinos, starting in 1898, when it colonised that island country....I could keep going all day long about massacres and genocide in Palestine, India, Asia, Africa the Americas, Oceania and Europe, during the last 500 years of Eurmerican colonialism, with whopping percentages of the local population decimated every time. The point is, in historical perspective, yes 4.6% of the Chinese population lost during the Great Leap Forward period is a tragedy, which Baba Beijing officially accepts. But it is by no means unusual, as an event nor in its magnitude."

Extremely well-said. Extremely rarely heard.

I'd like to add the Great Persian Famine of 1917-19 orchestrated by the British, which killed a minimum of 20% of our population and possibly as high as 50%. Ten million people died, making Iran actually the greatest victim of World War One. I bet you've never heard that view, either. Yet I defy you to find any English literature on the Persian Famine whatsoever - of course, you'll have no problem finding English-language scholarship on the Great Leap's famine as new works are always being written, published, reviewed in their Mainstream Media, advertised, etc.

Returning to the global famines perpetuated by colonialists – who attempted no Great Leaps Forward for the natives: Why is that we have no Western names or faces associated with these crimes, and yet Western schoolchildren are universally taught that Mao is a butcher? Were I to list the names of the persons in charge of Brown's modest list of genocides I would be listing the names of beloved Western heroes. The answer to this question is: apathy, ignorance, racism, hypocrisy, elitism but, absolutely above all, the total lack of the politically-modern view which can only be supplied via socialism.

All this proves, and as all leftist non-Westerners already know: Despite the fear-mongering over Mao (and Islam) it is Western capitalists who are by far the deadliest; despite the constant trumpeting of socialist misdeeds, it is the capitalists who have the guiltiest war machine. The only difference is that the Western Christian capitalists stay on message and practice propaganda / auto-critique much better.

Brown also bluntly encapsulates (and I understand his possible exasperation) the Chinese people's reaction to the Great Leap Forward's famine:

"In sum, did people die during the Great Leap Forward, due to droughts and flooding? Yes. As a result was there hunger and starvation? Yes. Did the masses blame the CPC, rise up and overthrow it. No."

And they absolutely could have because, as I mentioned, this was a postwar, battle-hardened society. Arms were all over, per Brown:

"Due to the Korean War, Taiwan, the CIA in Tibet and Western-fomented suicide missions, a village often had had 1-200 arms on hand until confiscations began in

the early 1980s."

Yet they did not have a popular (counter) revolution. So either the Westerners are right and the Chinese are just plain "*docile*", or they collectively decided to keep the Communist Party in power because they did enough (not all) things right? I'm sad to say that this is a crucial question for Westerners to pose themselves: Chinese "*docility*" – and other racist nonsense – has clearly formed a major part of their intellectual culture on this matter, and many others.

Therefore, it must finally be admitted that the Chinese Communist Party remains in power via democratic choice.

The problem with Westerners on this point is two-fold: consciously, it is probably not the choice they would democratically make for themselves right now, given their capitalist-imperialist leanings, and it is human nature to view our own choices as superior to others; subconsciously, they may often feel as though Westerners should be making the choices for the Chinese...still! The only way to resolve such cognitive and emotional issues is via new scholarship which shows the many errors of received Western "wisdom" on China.

Officially, the Chinese Communist Party openly says Mao was right 70% of the time and wrong 30% of the time. How rarely is this fact – universally-known in China – reported in the West?!

The Chinese themselves are clearly more honest than what you have likely read in the West on the Great Leap Forward, which is: the Great Leap Forward was 100% wrong, the famine was proof of its ideological / moral incorrectness, and that it did not even contribute to China's later economic success.

That is the view of an extremist.

I concede that mismanagement is a crime, and that mistakes were made during the Great Leap Forward, but I am no extremist: I say that the West is 90% wrong in their journalism, and 80% wrong in their academia.

It is a tough task to bring the West down from their perch of arrogant extremism on this subject – I hope this chapter has made a small contribution to that humane effort.

Ramin Mazaheri

3

When Chinese Trash saved the world - Western lies about the Cultural Revolution

*O*f the West's three main "Reasons Why Red China is Evil and the West is Morally & Ideologically Superior" propaganda campaign, the Cultural Revolution outranks the Great Leap Forward and the legacy of Mao for being far and away the most difficult for non-Chinese to truly get a handle on. Most leftists won't even touch it, much less defend it an inch...and thus they have completely ceded the entire era to socialism's Western ideological enemies for decades. Thus, it should be easily admitted and quite clear that we necessarily have been left with a completely one-sided portrayal of the Cultural Revolution.

And that's when we have a view at all! I would imagine that 9 out of every 10 Westerners can't truly say anything even a bit substantial about the Cultural Revolution. But for those who can repeat the West's propaganda, what's needed is to de-mythologize, to contextualise – historically, culturally, politically and relative to the rest of the 1960s world – and to defend the many ignored, obscured and simply unknown aims and achievements of the Cultural Revolution. It's a revolution, which truly needs a revolution in analysis; like all popular revolutions of the modern era – it has things to teach us about our own societies and everyone's modern times.

From the West's point of view there was certainly nothing to defend: Their view of the Cultural Revolution is that all free-thinking was attacked; supremely moral people were tarred and feathered; perfectly-intentioned and chaste schoolteachers were forced to wear dunce caps while sitting atop dunk tanks; chaos was official government policy; legislation entailed lunacies such as forcing compasses to rest pointing at south; cats and dogs were ordered to live together; and it only ended after the jaws of life were able to pry China from Mao's cold, dead hands.

The good news for the West is that their ignorance is not a risk, because such an event is culturally untranslatable – such a thing could never happen in the West, right? Sure, the West acknowledges the Chinese are capable in some ways – they aren't Blacks or Muslims – but there's still something fishy....

In the case of the Cultural Revolution Fairbank's exceptional, Harvard-backed acumen determined that the culprit was – in what some may view as a profound and deft intellectual summation of a lifetime of studying the Middle Kingdom – the fundamentally, intractably, universally "*passive*" character of the Chinese. He posits in his opening remarks in his chapter on the Cultural Revolution:

"In looking at the Cultural Revolution (CR) in China, we are therefore obliged to imagine a society that can be run by a Great Leader and a party dictatorship simply because the citizenry are passive in politics and obedient to authority. They have no human rights because they have been taught that the assertion of human rights (such as due process of law) would be selfish and antisocial and therefore ignoble."

It's tough to be Chinese...docile, passive, obedient, apparently totally lawless, and even uncomprehending of human rights (any of them). I would have thought that every society contained at least one single human right...but no – Harvard's Fairbank says they have "no human rights". And it's funny how they went from installing a massive, modern, socialist revolution to passive in just around 15 years?

But who are we to judge? Fairbank's *New York Times* obituary impressively begins: "John K. Fairbank, the Harvard history professor who was widely credited with creating the field of modern Chinese studies in the United States..." And yet there can be no doubt that his above-quoted paragraph is pure nonsense, clearly racist and terribly unacademic. It could be considered a success in one view: it is excellent propaganda, as it inspires shock, abhorrence, self-pride, anti-intellectualism, anti-socialism and extremism among Western readers.

When a culture's most esteemed teachings about China's Cultural Revolution are based on a foundation which essentially equate to – "first we must envision the Chinese as humans who do not appreciate humanity" – we must read such teachings with extreme caution, and then search for better analysis of this important modern historical period. But let's not forget how standard these faulty foundations are in Western academia: read their studies of Mao, Stalin, Khomeini, Khamenei, the Castros or any anti-imperialist, and – from the base of their pyramid to their "doyens" like Fairbank – these heroes to billions are consistently reduced to being non-humans. That is why anyone who publicly says "I understand them" must be screwed up in the head. Open sympathy may land you in jail, or at least fired.

It is certain that we cannot keep blindly accepting such mainstream nonsense about China's recent socialist past, and fail to learn about possible Chinese solutions to universal problems. That would make you rather *"obedient"* and *"passive"* – are part Chinese or something?

The true educational aim of the Cultural Revolution: Finally, give Chinese Trash a chance

We have no choice but to start at zero with primary sources:

"The task of the Cultural Revolution is to reform the old education system and education philosophy and methodology." – Chinese Communist Party's Central Committee, May 16 Directive (1966), which initiated the Cultural Revolution.

Due to its total historical exclusion in the West, I must first address the primary yet studiously ignored aspect of the Cultural Revolution: granting mass rural education for the first time.

Above all, the explicit "task" of Cultural Revolution was a revolution in education, and it is this new inclusion of rural voices which naturally revolutionised the urban-dominated post-1949 culture, causing inevitable friction. Indeed, this is the thesis from which to operate: By opening up China's overall national education / culture to rural Chinese Trash, that necessarily produced conflict with the hitherto urban-dominated communist culture, and the hard-won victory of Chinese Trash is what is now appropriately termed a "Cultural Revolution".

Another, more universal, thesis is this: If one fails to acknowledge the intensity of the urban-rural divide – which is a universal byproduct of the industrial era – one cannot understand the Chinese Cultural Revolution, nor recognise its immediate necessity for a parallel overhaul in the West.

But this original aim must be hidden: Denying that the Cultural Revolution actually represented a vast increase in education is a primary propaganda tactic of the West on this issue. Thusly, Fairbank denigrates one of the Cultural Revolution's totally ignored yet absolutely primary programs – the rural education program – as mere "*indoctrination*"...and he leaves it at that! (In a similar vein but with the opposite tack, you can find plenty of Western propaganda about the alleged "failure" of socialist Cuba's famous literacy drive.)

But demanding equal education opportunities is surely the sign of a modern democrat, and Brown refuses Fairbank's dishonesty, willful blindness and baseline suspicion:

"The other aspect about the Cultural Revolution was Mao's ardent desire to bring rural education out of the dark ages. After 1949, the education system the education system improved dramatically for urbanites, as well as for illiterate adults....But for farm folk, the education system changed little after liberation. It was still controlled by urban, intellectual elites, who largely scorned the hundreds of millions of peasants in the countryside....The Cultural Revolution changed all that."

The invaluable benefit of sympathetic, open-minded, 21st-century scholars like Brown is that he is open to the Chinese view of China's history, rather than rewriting it in order to promote Western ideology. Not only is Brown embedded in Chinese society, but he is willing to use modern Chinese sources, such as Dongping Han, who wrote the immensely necessary book, *The Unknown Cultural Revolution: Life and Change in a Chinese Village*. Westerners, and especially journalists, mostly only talk to those who fled China and bear a grudge. It's the same thing when it comes to Iran, but I shouldn't complain – the anti-Castro faction has far more political power in Florida than the Iranian monarchy's ex-elites in Beverly Hills and around Washington D.C.

We must keep in mind just how much the West has lacked new or different ideas, analyses and facts on the Cultural Revolution: this is an intellectual battle where Western leftists have long since quit the field, while Chinese expatriate leftists have rarely been present in the West long enough to raise their voice or to be heard. Thinkers like Dongping Han, a professor in the United States, are truly the first of this kind. Given the sustained success of the People's Republic, they certainly will not be the last.

Han's facts are undeniably weighty, and must be accounted for when discussing the Cultural Revolution: in 1966, the start of the Cultural Revolution, his village of 1,300 students had 8 middle schools and 2 high schools. When it was over, his county had 249 middle schools and 89 high schools. In 1966, 65 percent of all rural schools had no desks and chairs, but by the end of the Cultural Revolution, per Brown, *"To say that the Cultural Revolution radically improved the educational foundation of rural China would be a gross understatement."*

And to *"radically improve the educational foundation of rural"* society, is thus to improve all of society. However, it must be retained in mind that mass rural education was seemingly unknown to humanity for our 5,000 years of recorded history, and thus this modern development can affect a national culture in unpredicted ways.

If there's one thing a capitalist is, it's impatient. They are simply appalled that any Socialist-inspired revolution has taken more than one week to succeed...and this is why capitalists are such bad political leaders – real changes take longer than a financial quarter. But if we look at a timeline of Chinese Communist Party governance: After reversing foreign domination and exploitation (1927-49), then assuring domestic security (Korean War, 1950-53), and then having boosted urban education and teaching the illiterate, the time came to raise up the rural areas via education.

Of course, when rural citizens have achieved equal educational levels they will insist on and deserve equal say in the overall national culture...and - spoiler alert – newly empowered Chinese peasants did NOT want a gradual return to capitalism via "revisionism".

In a very real sense, which Iranians will understand easily: rural "conservatives" in China had very often become truer revolutionaries. Many urbanites became increasingly viewed as the more easily corruptible cadres, more easily swayed from the revolutionary path and more easily swayed from the national / cultural morality. The explanation is partially due to class: the rural area was a class segment, which still had not been assured of basic needs (education, empowerment, etc.)... and they wanted them!

This is the polar opposite of the West, where urbanites in 2018 – in the aftermath of Brexit and the election of Donald Trump - view rural areas as useless, dead-weight, burdensome trash (note my lack of a capital 'T'). A "hillbilly progressive", much less a "hillbilly revolutionary" is an oxymoron to the West – it is only "hillbilly reactionary" (although the West never uses "reactionary", as that comes from the vocabulary of leftism). However, this anti-rural prejudice is not a "universal value", and it is clearly wrong to assume this was the case in mid-60's China. And yet: how many Western White Trash have a similarly negative view of their nation's urbanites as the conservative-yet-revolutionary 1960s-era rural Chinese?

I hope we are beginning to see the scope of the problem – just how universal and modern it is - and also how China addressed this issue 50 years earlier! Acknowledging this problem – that the only democratic choice is to force rural citizens onto a cultural / educational / societal par with urbanites – is a major step to realising the major goal of the Cultural Revolution: ending the urban / rural divide.

And this is a good place to remind us that "Cultural Revolution" is a Western abbreviation: Great Proletarian Cultural Revolution is the official Chinese name, because this is when Maoism became "Maoism" culturally & nationally by making the rural people at least the equal of their Soviet godmen-proletariat / socialist forerunners: factory workers. In 1968 the Great Proletarian Cultural Revolution was placing rural on par with urban, uniting the proletariat in greater emphasis than ever before in a cultural sense.

The reality – still unperceived by many Western leftists today – is that urban factory workers having significantly higher education (and thus higher possible capability for modern political intelligence) than the average person was drastically reduced worldwide after WWII. Factory workers were a vanguard in 1917 Russia, but times change, and often rapidly. In 2018 it is a totally, totally, totally outdated concept that rural people are culturally or politically stupid, because we are all watching the same TV, internet, books, newspapers, media, etc. A huge step in ending rural isolation / increasing equality of media in the United States goes all the way back to Rural Free Delivery of mail in 1902 – it may not seem like much today, but we must remember what conditions prevailed before, and for so long. We must also always remember that politics and economics are moral issues - and thus easily understandable - certainly not technocratic. On top of it all, the idea that knowing how to run a machine is "education" but how to run a farm is not is a stupid, uniformed and prejudiced idea…and farmers are happy to watch you try and make it look easy).

Anti-rural prejudice has been truly as burdensome upon human society as is our long history of anti-female discrimination…and that is big. The

Cultural Revolution was – whether one condones or condemns it – certainly at least an effort to right this perpetual historical wrong.

Returning to education, it is certainly true that China did rob Peter to pay Paul: urban areas schools were closed for intermittent periods in 1966-70, but it was not the decade the West often falsely claims. Regardless, the urban closures must be mitigated by the undeniable fact that always too-limited education resources were poured into the rural areas during these closures.

It is not a coincidence that today we see that this is the exact opposite of French President Emmanuel Macron's education plan, which will close rural classes in order to put the money towards urban areas. French Trash is up in arms, of course, but what is never admitted is Macron's true goal, which is the same as the ruling elite's has always been: only being bothered to create a technocratic, self-censoring, self-aggrandising, urban elite in order to protect the elite of the elite. Rural values are certainly the opposite of Rothschild banker values

(Macron's previous employer); the 1% may own the land, but they don't have to work it like a j-o-b.

Furthermore in France, and showing the top-to-bottom American-style changes Macron is rapidly forcing through (often by executive decree, despite controlling parliament, in order to avoid public debate), is the...no, not the labor code rollback, the right-wing immigration bill, the normalisation of the state of emergency, the rail privatization, but his university education changes. It rarely got reported internationally but dozens of universities were closed by massive university protests in the Spring of 2018. Students, teachers, unions and parents are upset that, to quote a protester from one of my PressTV reports: *"Macron's university reforms are going to create a system where people from the rich, elite high schools in Paris are going to go to university more often than those from small cities and rural areas. It will mark the end of our system of equally encouraging everyone to pursue higher education."* The French say "Once does not make a custom", but this is two clear steps towards re-creating a technocratic urban elite, and moving away from democratising higher education for everyone.

What is undeniable is that, as Brown repeatedly relates, the rural people of China remember the Cultural Revolution fondly, even if urbanites do not; and even if the urban elites who fled the Cultural Revolution do not, especially when speaking to anti-socialist journalists in their new adopted countries.

But the West does not relay voices like Brown or Han – they only decry the mistakes of the Cultural Revolution, while steadfastly refusing to acknowledge the solutions and great leap-advances, such as in rural education.

The true reforming aim of the Cultural Revolution: Admitting revolutionary failure

We must realize that the 1949 Communist Revolution can be fairly called "merely" an anti-imperialist one, much like the 1776 United States Revolution: even if a new elite drawn from the regular People replaced the old, the same feudal mentality existed among the mass of the People.

China's Cultural Revolution changed all that. Indeed, it is truly the case that China's Trash Revolution did not fully arrive until their Cultural Revolution. The reason is something no Westerner will object to discussing about Red China: corruption and mismanagement.

Clearly, the West's "talented tenth" is rightly terrified of a Cultural Revolution happening in their own nations. The idea that they could be toppled from their comfortable perch, be tried for their corruption-related and anti-social crimes, or that they are not doing a fabulous job of leading the masses – is something they necessarily have to resist. Their power is based on their exclusivity and their alleged exceptionalism – just like a corrupt Chinese communist cadre – not on a broad social ideal or actual democratic mandate, whether formal or informal.

By the mid-1960s the Communist Party had been in charge for 15 years, and yet utopia was not quite at hand (surely the capitalists would have implemented that by 1960, had they been given the chance). From Fairbank:

*"As this effort continued (*the building up of China*), however, Mao became concerned about the seemingly inevitable buildup of the institutions of the central government and its many levels of officials and cadres who seemed to be taking the place of the local elite of imperial times. He feared a revival of the ruling-class domination of the villagers. Given the modern tendency for expert management, and the irrepressible tendency toward personal privilege and corruption among China's new ruling class, it would be hard to prove him wrong."*

(Obviously, we should ignore his parenthetical implication that only China's new socialist ruling class had a tendency towards corruption – Faribank gives no proof or reason why the Chinese are more corrupt than anyone else.)

What is truthful is that modern 20th century history shows that technocratism – "expert management" – is indeed a major threat to the average person: Hillary Clinton was the "most qualified presidential candidate ever", while

Brussels is built on the altar of technocratism. What is never said in Western media is the primary fault with these oh-so "qualified" people: their neoliberal, neo-imperialist ideology is terrible and clearly unwanted democratically.

But Fairbank makes clear – and you wouldn't believe me if I hadn't quoted him – the basis of the Mao-led Cultural Revolution was to preserve the most anti-oligarchic aspects of the 1949 Revolution, because exchanging one minor gentry for another ("imperial gentry" replaced by "communist gentry") is no revolution at all but a brand change – it's like going from Dubya to Obama.

Brown confirms Mao had the same goal, but with more honesty and without implications against Chinese society. Brown notes that Mao had already launched 7 anti-corruption campaigns between 1951-65, and yet he was quoted in 1964 as openly saying: *"At present you can buy a Party branch secretary for a few packs of cigarettes, not to mention marrying a daughter to him."*

Westerners assume that such honesty

cannot exist in socialist-inspired countries: those places are all totalitarian spy states, right? They have no conception of the range of government critiques in Iranian media, either. But the Chinese know better, and they knew that in the mid-60s, which is why Mao openly admitted it. Back to Fairbank:

"The (August 1966 Eleventh) *plenum also put forward Mao's general vision of the moment against revisionism, which was intended to achieve a drastic change in the mental outlook of the whole Chinese people. Spiritual regeneration, as he put it, was to take precedence over economic development."*

Fairbank, as a Western intellectual, must of course cast doubt on the very idea that the Eleventh plenum was possibly the product of a democratic discussion process which involved more than just Mao's ideas; perhaps far more important is his Wester academic duty to cast proper doubt on anything known as "spiritual regeneration", much less a socialist-inspired one. What another crazy idea of that soulless monster Mao – spiritual development over economic development!

Regardless, the core of the problem was the Communist Party being so ineffective. Therefore, the Cultural Revolution was the attempt by the many honest revolutionaries of the Party to appeal to grassroots power, instead of the Party apparatus or even the People's Liberation Army. Per Brown:

"So the Cultural Revolution was Mao's exasperated ploy to clean up and clear out the Party, with the help of the citizens, by giving them the authority to stand up, be heard and punish and/or remove the millions of rotten local cadres who were mostly making their lives miserable and poorer."

Fairbank and the West are incapable – or unwilling – to view the Cultural Revolution from this perspective: the bottom, the 99%, the People. If they did, they clearly would see that Brown's analysis – that the Cultural Revolution empowered the average person over the establishment of the Communist Party – exonerates the Cultural Revolution in terms of its clear pro-democratic aims.

Part of Fairbank's problem is that the Chinese take corruption (good governance) very seriously and without that *film noir*, cynical tolerance of Western modernity – they execute people over it (like in Iran). The West views governance as a path to self-enrichment, or an obstacle to self-enrichment, and thinks they are more moral than the Chinese because their bribery is done in the sunshine and called "lobbying". Despite all the scandals during France's administrations of Sarkozy and Hollande – nobody has ever gone to prison, nor likely will.

It is also not unfair to point out that when the West says that the Cultural Revolution was an attempt to consolidate power, factionalism, or the killing off of dissidents, it must be remembered that many of these dissidents were the West's ideological allies, as they composed the ones who did not want corruption to be rooted out – they were the corrupt ones, in what surely must have been a significant percentage of cases. They say that everyone in jail claims to be innocent – I can promise you that every Iranian regime refugee says they were pure angels, the most devoted of public servants and that "the other guy" was the corrupt one.

What were the "show trials" of the Cultural Revolution, after all? They were, apart from the top-level ones, mostly "trial by a jury of your peers": if you were a small-time cadre running a small-time factory in a small-time town…your workers and the townspeople knew, by your years of actions, if you needed to be tarred and feathered and run out of town or not, no? Are small-town hicks even so stupid that they don't know what is really going on in their own hick town? I doubt it but, regardless of what I think, the Cultural Revolution empowered locals to make these decisions with a base question of: "Corrupt, or not corrupt?" This is not an exoneration of a lynch-mob, but to deny the accusation that the Cultural Revolution was nothing but unfair, illogical, lynch-mob justice as the West often claims.

Did unjust things happen in the Cultural Revolution? Yes. Simply Google that term and you will find plenty of examples, some of which are likely true, so you don't need my input on that subject. This book is to provide balance to the critics of the Cultural Revolution, which is all that exists in the West.

Was it all Mao or the Communist Party's fault? Absolutely not, and that's even according to Fairbank: *"To be sure, as the situation got increasingly out of control and into violence, Mao made various efforts to rein it in, but seldom successfully."*

I appreciate Fairbank's even-handedness here, but mismanagement is still a crime… in China at least. However, mismanagement is not the same as a "policy of genocide/fear/chaos" that the West usually portrays as the motivation for and guiding policy of the Cultural Revolution.

Given that rural education was nonexistent and that the Party had become non-revolutionary, we should ask: how can a culture truly change for the better?

The true societal aim of the Cultural Revolution: A revolution in mentality, or it's not 'revolution'

How did Mao give the people *"the authority to stand up"*, as Brown wrote?

There is another reason this dramatic

policy had to occur, which Fairbank describes but which Brown gets at much better: the Cultural Revolution undermined the Confucian-inspired ideals which were the longtime basis of Chinese culture.

Why was this needed? For those who are unfamiliar with Confucius, let's just say that the emphasis is on knowing your role and fulfilling your duties, and not "damn the societal costs-individualism" of the West.

We can debate all day about how much more "obedient" the Chinese are than, say, the Germans, who seem to follow authority pretty darn blindly in recent decades… but isn't it already clear what an absurd discussion this is? It's obvious to intelligent people that one nation is not more or less obedient than another – such discussions are reactionary and full of inaccuracies. Therefore, obedience to undeserved temporal authority is something, which requires a revolution everywhere.

We have seen that even Mao openly insulted the corruption of Communist Party cadres, but China – just like seemingly everywhere in the 1950s – was a rather conservative place. People did not buck established postwar authorities, and the Communist Party had earned the right to become "established". Indeed, the idea that China's postwar experience – and China was the 2nd-biggest victim of WWII, closely behind the USSR – was somehow *radically different from the rest of the world's*, even amid an increasingly connected globe, is a common blind spot for the West. The 60's would be a "crazy time" for China for the same reason it was crazy almost everywhere else in the world.

But it is with this open encouragement to buck authority, which reminds us yet again what an intensely true revolutionary – what a true friend of the People – Mao really was. Brown neatly elucidates the Chinese cultural & political context of a revolution threatened by diminishing revolutionary ideals (this continues with Brown's last quote, from the previous section of this chapter, about giving the People the authority to stand up to corruption.):

"They were the victims of this official abuse and they were the ones who could fix

the problem. If only they could overcome their fear and feudal subservience, then the crooks could be overwhelmed and not be able to protect each other and themselves.

Westerners scoff at Mao's backers supporting the anti-Lin Biao & Confucius campaign as being frivolous, but they completely miss the point. Mao was giving hundreds of millions of timid, cowed masses the opportunity to stand up and vocally criticise two of the country's icons, one modern and one ancient. It was a set piece for the people to practice throwing off their feudal mindset and speak with a collective voice of authority and conviction."

In the mid-1960s it was clear that – were the Revolution to not just survive but to keep advancing towards greater equality, justice and individual empowerment – removing corrupt government workers / societal leaders was a must. So there is no doubt why corrupt Party leaders, bad teachers, etc. lost their privileged status: actions were to be judged, regardless of status, job titles, degrees, etc. The West focuses on the miscarriages of justice, which demand restitution, but certainly not the whole picture of the Cultural Revolution.

Perhaps Westerners prefer to hear it in their own terms: Just imagine if Henry Kissinger or Rachel Maddow had to face a crowd of everyday people who were governmentally-empowered to judge their ideological and real crimes? Kissinger could only get exonerated if the trial was held on Wall Street or in the Pentagon, that's for sure. Who wouldn't love to see Maddow cleaning latrines – why is she above an immigrant cleaning lady? Why is cleaning bathrooms or rural work a demeaning job, to begin with? Maybe Obama has never been paid to clean toilets and thought "Where's MY bailout?", but I have and it certainly shaped my political views for the better. Maybe the perspective of the West's "talented tenth" would improve if they changed their cultural throne for the porcelain one for a long spell?

Clearly, the West's "talented tenth" is terrified of such a thing happening – capitalists love comfort, after all.

Above all, this is why the Cultural Revolution is covered in propaganda – what cultural / social leader is going to green-light this version of it, much less take this angle in every news item? This is why we never hear the positives of the Cultural Revolution, but we can now, thanks to people like Brown:

"The leadership should be rightfully fearful of the people, not the other way around; a great definition of participatory democracy... Thus, the Party had better work its butt off to make sure those who would sell out the communist revolution for a few crumbs of Western empire, are rid of, or at least neutralized.

In the West, it is depicted that this went on for years. In fact, the majority of the vandalism happened during a brief six-week period in the summer of 1966. They did do a lot of damage in such a short period of time and the leadership quickly sent out the People's Liberation Army to stop it. It was one of the big reasons that Mao, soon thereafter, sent these city youths into the countryside, for rural education... It was a great way to get these overzealous kids out of the cities and take some starch out of them. In fact, it worked like a charm. The rural education program for city slickers is still highly valued win China."

The 1960s were a crazy time worldwide… but I think we can say that the May 1968 protests in France or the anti-Vietnam War protests in the US did have some positive societal effects, no? Yet China's domestic uprisings were 100% negative? Obviously a case of one weight, two measures (to improve on a bad French proverb).

Again, would it be fair of the Chinese to say: "There can be no doubt that the West's 1960s protests were all an abominable, undemocratic atrocity" – as the West does about China? Of course not… but this is more proof of the false reality promoted by Western media and academics on the Cultural Revolution.

A revolution in mentality was needed, or the revolution would have been short-lived…and the Chinese are fond of their Revolution. Per Brown:

"To this day, knowledgeable people inside and outside China say that the Cultural Revolution brought long lasting, badly needed changes to the mindset of the Chinese masses."

The true political aim of the Cultural Revolution: Reducing, not increasing, Mao's power

I hope we are beginning to see that the Cultural Revolution was actually a devolving of power away from the powerful and the establishment, in a fulfilment of socialist ideals.

And yet Westerners are told that it was all an effort by Mao to sideline his competition. Perhaps more than any of these false Western claims, I am rather boggled at the preponderance of evidence against this idea.

I understand that the idea that an establishment party would willfully threaten itself with destruction via self-criticism is impossible for the West to comprehend. Truly, for a Western politician threatened with losing re-election there is no political deal or moral compromise too shady.

Perhaps that is why the Cultural Revolution is portrayed as the misguided whim of a dictator. The underlying theme seemingly is: "Lacking reasons or justifications is simply what socialists always do, because they are totalitarian". On cue, Fairbank:

"Only if we regard him (Mao) as a monarch in succession to scores of emperors can we imagine why the leadership of the CCP, trained to be loyal, went along with his piecemeal assault and destruction of them."

Fairbank believes that the Cultural Revolution is just "the Chinese being Chinese". This is lazy and racist, but it's also historical nihilism because it posits that there can be no new, revolutionary ethical / political motivations despite the changing circumstances of life / culture.

And yet Fairbank, because he is writing a textbook, must make a cursory list of the facts, even though he is not obligated to incorporate them into his analysis. These facts clearly prove the progressive, democratic, egalitarian nature and aims of the Cultural Revolution, the Chinese Communist Party and Mao himself – which I will list because if I paraphrased I would not have been believed:

(To avoid grammatical alterations to the quote, please keep in mind that

Fairbank is writing to illustrate Mao's dissatisfied view of China in the mid-1960s.)

"But what did Mao think he was doing? Perhaps it can be summed up as an effort to make 'democratic centralism' more democratic and centralist. He saw the new bureaucracy following the ancient pattern of autocratic government from the top down. This would leave the peasant masses where they had always been, at the bottom of society, being exploited by a new elite... Local decisions should not all depend on Beijing bureaucrats. The aim of government should be the welfare and indoctrination of the local peasant masses...."

Fairbank again shows his urban snobbery: he assumes that rural people are so easy to "*indoctrinate*".

I pity Fairbank, because somewhere in his mind he knew that Mao's aim was clearly to promote democracy, clearly against the consolidation of power in Beijing via centralization, clearly for the welfare of rural citizens...and yet to say that openly would have been career and social suicide. Yet Fairbank has to mention Mao's true aims, as he is a historian, even if he refuses to expound on them or take them seriously.

Mao took on the establishment in a myriad of ways instead of strengthening the establishment, which he led. Mao encouraged the Red Guards (the newly created revolution student organization) to take on the "capitalist roaders" in the army. Truly, what kind of "dictator" sides with students over soldiers? Furthermore, this shows how democratic and not dictatorial Mao was: if he had lost the support of the army, he surely risked being victimised by a military coup.

By taking on the People's Liberation Army, Mao was able to create revolutionary committees everywhere to allow local, democratic reassessment of revolutionary progress. When the Red Guards had shocked the stagnant urbanites sufficiently, he sent them to the country, and Fairbank's Western urban snobbishness is again in full view:

"The dispersal of the Red Guards led to their being sent down in large numbers to the countryside, casting them from the heights of political importance to the depths."

One is sure that the fake-leftists of the West today still view the countryside as "*the depths*", sadly for them. Again, the urban / rural divide is not new – what is new is Mao's placing the mantle of proletarian leadership upon them. Of course, placing such a mantle was perhaps inevitable: Chinese elevation of farmers is not at all new to them, even if it is a foreign concept in the 21st-century West.

By 1969 a new wave in the PLA had replaced the old bureaucrats. Many Westerners believe this was a regression of some sort: I say better a modern, socialist-inspired soldier than a corrupt bureaucrat who acts like an entrepreneurial merchant and creates an undemocratic Deep State.

But I hope we are in agreement: it is impressive how very democratic and socialist the Cultural Revolution truly was: Decentralization, democratization, taking on the Party establishment, taking on the intellectual class, the urban class, the *nouvelle riche* class, the army class – all were attacked with demands to reform politically and morally. And I have barely mentioned his relationship with the student / youth class, which requires serious re-assessment!

So how can the Cultural Revolution be Mao's dictatorial power grab when he is siding against all the entrenched classes? I'll tell you how: only by rewriting history and forbidding dissenting views, which is what the West has done.

What was the West doing in the 1960s? Dropping out & corrupting in - repressing, not unchaining, their youth

For me the defining motif of the Cultural Revolution is this absolutely incredible and supremely admirable fact: In 1966 – at a time when Mao likely could have grabbed more power for himself due to his success, experience and stature – he willingly threw in his lot with the youth! He actually devolved and decentralised power down to the youth and told them that they should guide and motivate the revolution now, and not his generation. What a romantic revolutionary, no?!

Who in the West – what leader actually in power – did that in the 1960s?

None did – it was always the opposite. Mao has provided an example, which truly forces one to re-evaluate one's concept of revolutionary commitment in myriad ways.

The Cultural Revolution actually proved Mao to be the most in-tune popular leader of his time: he saw that the youth were rebelling, understood the reasons why and what they wanted, and he was the only top leader who encouraged them in a positive political direction.

Mao did this in 1966, when the concept of a Great Proletarian Cultural Revolution was being debated and formulated by China's intellectuals (Iran's Cultural Revolution was the same: the product of years of public debate, and not some bewildering order dictated from high above.)

Following the May 16 Directive and in the same month, a female 45-year old philosophy teacher at Beijing University – surely along with sympathetic teachers and students – put up on campus the first-ever large font poster: it openly condemned university leadership for being revisionists, anti-socialists and oppressors of students. Maybe in the West one wouldn't be fired or expelled for this...but only "maybe". What's unthinkable is that a Western head of state would promote this attack on such an entrenched class of the establishment. Yet the protest sign came to Mao's attention and that's exactly what he did. Mao rebroadcast it widely, and responded to the "hip" new communication method by joining it – with his own famous large-font poster, "Bombard the Headquarters". (I imagine "Bombard" is a willfully-bad English translation, much as chants in Iran of "Death to...(America, England, the MEK/MKO cult of "hypocrites" & Israel, usually) are better translated as "Down with....")

Mao emphatically supported the students and their new ideas based on revolutionary purity and virtue. By July millions had spontaneously created and joined the newly-formed Red Guards, all without central organisation. Clearly, the Red Guards had a grassroots, democratic beginning.

August 1966 saw the first of eight

million-person rallies at Tiananmen Square in favor of launching the Cultural Revolution. Mao donned their uniform and joined them there. Fuelled with Mao's seemingly unthinkable anti-establishment slogans like "It is Right to Rebel", the Cultural Revolution was off and running.

If this all seems completely foreign to the Western historical experience, that's because it is: I am totally unaware of a top leader – not a fringe intellectual, not an occasional professor – telling his Western nation's students that it is "right to rebel". I'd be surprised if Western baby boomers do not feel slightly jealous at the way this Chinese generation of youth and students were empowered, trusted, given prominence and given the power to effect real political change.

It should be really quite startling - the scope and the revolutionary risk of it all: trusting students to help topple a corrupted chunk of the establishment. But to Mao and the true Party members it was not a risk but a duty, because – as the grassroots, democratic nature of the Cultural Revolution movement cannot be questioned – socialist democracy means that true believers support such anti-rightist movements.

The idea of handing power to the students is indeed revolutionary – this is why France suppressed the 1968 May revolt and why Iran's mullahs encouraged their students: one did not want revolution, the other did. It is unthinkable that students in 21st century France would have fought to support the Sarkozy, Hollande or Macron administrations, to give just one Western example, and that shows just how unique (revolutionary) China's government was in the 1960s.

We should see that the 1960s were, "The '60s, man!" in China as well as in the West…but what very different paths they chose. While the West was experiencing rebellion against what they perceived as puritanism – hating their parents, using drugs to gain cheap spirituality, being sexually promiscuous – their Chinese peers were experiencing a rebirth of revolutionary puritanism. The West's results, several decades later, appear evident: even more rampant drug use with even stronger pharmaceutical self-centred spirituality instead of rule-based, society-centered religion; 40% of children in the US are born to unmarried mothers with 25% of children raised without a father. The Chinese baby boomers are not without sin, but they don't have these society- and culture-destroying phenomena – the Communists ended their Opium Wars, after all…

And how quickly did the Western baby boomers become apolitical after their ruckuses in the 1960s? Did that generation of youth not quickly embrace neoliberal capitalism and support the rollback of decades of socialist-inspired achievements won by their ancestors? And yet how enduring has Chinese socialism been?

How different the West might be today if they had empowered their revolutionary baby boomer youth? That is a useless question, sadly, but the Chinese have their answer, and it is thanks to the revolutionary commitment of Mao and his colleagues. Indeed, comparing Chinese and Western baby boomers is not a fair race: the Chinese had such a huge head start, in terms of access to and familiarity with modern political intelligence.

Cultural wars aside, we simply need to remember that China does not live in a cultural vacuum – the 1960s were crazy worldwide – and also that China does not live in a political vacuum either. Few consider the Cultural Revolution in the context of a response to the recent and very threatening Americanisation of the Vietnam War: Without the revolutionary spirit needed to galvanise Chinese support...well, China appeared quite obviously to be next on the chopping block.

What's certainly never mentioned in the West is that in 1965 the US was also significantly aiding the destruction of the world's largest communist power not in power – in Indonesia - even though it meant the death of 3 million people. Extremist anti-socialists in Washington were obviously hell-bent on massacring as many as possible to restore capitalist imperialism worldwide in the new US order.

Given these very real threats, who can say the Cultural Revolution was not needed, and also quite possibly far less bloody than a 1960s China without the

Cultural Revolution but which was being invaded? It is the journalist in me which rejects Monday-morning quarterbacking and which repeatedly asks: What actually were the realistic possibilities at the time when decisions were forced to be made? Invasion certainly appeared realistic in 1960s China. Invasion in 2018 America, for example, is not remotely likely, so anyone who talks about that is spouting nonsense. Therefore, the Chinese were absolutely right to re-revolutionize in order to prevent another "century of humiliation".

The situation among China's political allies is also rarely considered in discussions of the necessity of the Cultural Revolution. They were clearly just as bad in the mid-1960s, and not just in Indochina: Mao declared his independence from the USSR a decade earlier with the Great Leap's new economic focus, but he rightly perceived that corruption was taking firm root in the birthplace of socialism. Even Fairbank has to give a grudging approval to Mao's obviously democratic view of the 1960s USSR:

"In the USSR Mao saw 'revisionism' at

work, that is, a falling away from egalitarian concern for the people and their collective organisation and instead the growth of a new ruling class of specially privileged, urban-centred, and technically educated people who were kept in line, like the populace in general, by the powerful secret police. Given the West's general appraisal of the Soviet dictatorship, Mao's distrust can hardly be faulted."

It's a common and credible belief – both in 1968 and in 2018 – that a large reason for the ultimate failure of the USSR was because of their Communist Party's failure to have a corruption-weeding Cultural Revolution of their own. Instead of a Cultural Revolution, they had the calm-but-regressive Brezhnev era (1964-82). Stagnation produces creeping counter-revolutionaries, as evidenced by the toleration and then promotion of people like Gorbachev, with a Parliament-bombing Yeltsin the inevitable step.

The Cultural Revolution's legacy: More proof today's success is because of it, not in spite of it

"Living here for 13 years and knowing that these days there are 300-500 daily public protests against the system, in reality, against the CPC, this kind of popular vigilance would never have reached fruition without the Cultural Revolution's baptism by populist fire."

If that level of participatory democracy described by Brown is present because of the Cultural Revolution...it obviously succeeded beyond Mao's grandest hopes, no? That is the exact opposite of *"At present you can buy a Party branch secretary for a few packs of cigarettes,"* because the Chinese people are vigilant, demanding and bold now.

I can promise you from experience that such statistics will never get past Western media editors. France has 10 protests per day, for example, and it is considered the most protest-happy nation by the Anglo-Saxon world. (Of course, as Chapter 1 proved, China is a continent, while France is just a nation. Proportionally speaking, France is about half as politically demonstrative as China.)

Economic policy is always cultural – this is why it's absolutely false to believe the West's assertion that the era of the Cultural Revolution made no contribution to China's current economic success, military security and stability. Per Brown:

"Just as Mao Zedong's amazing socioeconomic miracle from 1949-1978 was critical for Deng Xiaopeng's later reforms to succeed, it can be persuasively argued that the 1966-1976 Cultural Revolution was just as necessary, for the Chinese people to develop the attitude and sense of social justice needed to implement these incredible changes and make them happen."

Contrary to the tear gas I am routinely forced to flee at anti-government demonstrations in Paris – China's government realizes that workers & citizens bringing problems to public attention actually increases efficiency by rectifying wrongs, increasing satisfaction and giving management the truth from the factory floor and public streets. The Cultural Revolution can be seen as a sort of multi-year demonstration.

In a very clear way the Cultural Revolution proved to Washington that they had no chance to win back the China they had "lost" – the Communist Party was firmly in charge, and nothing was going to change that anymore: not Vietnam, not Korea nor lingering domestic subversion. Nixon restored relations in 1972, and China has not looked over their shoulder in fear since.

This chapter has focused on the technical, historical and analytical aspects of the Cultural Revolution, but I think it's obvious just how applicable their situation is to the West today. There is no question that populism has risen greatly in the West in 2018, and hopefully we now see that it is of a sort which has many obvious, if unexpected, cultural parallels to 1960s China. These parallels are so clear and so important that Chapter 5 is devoted to examining them.

Beijing officially admits the Cultural Revolution was a mistake... not because it was *in toto*, but because that is the only way to move on – every good parent knows this. They have officially apologised to all the victims and instituted reparations programs. China clearly has few problems discussing it openly.

In the end, the Cultural Revolution

was an anti-1%, Trash Revolution, Revolution of the Barefooted – no wonder the West cannot discuss it with anything but 100%-negative extremism.

4
Mao's legacy defended, and famous swim decoded, for clueless academics

*T*here is a great story about Mao at the very start of the Cultural Revolution, which is well-known but which has been seemingly universally mystifying. Nobody in the West has been able to make sense of it - ever - but I think that's because they lacked the spiritual tools. I think I have finally discovered the moral behind Mao's actions.

In late 1965 the rumblings of the Cultural Revolution had begun, due to grumblings over corruption, revisionism, technocratism and urban conceit. The party, led by Mao, saw these trends as threats to the common good, the revolution, and the Party's "Heavenly Mandate" – the millennia-old concept that China's rulers are chosen by Heaven to rule, and that they must actually display this divinity via perfectly moral conduct and leadership...or else revolt becomes justified.

Mao, being the great progressive leader he was, was against these anti-socialist trends, but there was only so much he could do about it on his own. His seven anti-corruption campaigns since 1949 had not been sufficiently successful: the problem was deeply embedded, and beyond the reach of one man – even if one assumes Mao to be the totalitarian "Mao the Terrible" the West portrays him as.

With decades of anti-imperialist and anti-capitalist fighting clearly under threat from domestic reactionaries, in 1966 Mao supervised the Party's May 16 Directive to unmask the goals of this counter-revolutionary threat: *"... they will seize political power and turn the dictatorship of the proletariat into a dictatorship of the bourgeoisie."* Decoded: the corrupt pro-capitalists will turn China into a West European (bourgeois) democracy.

And from a foreign policy perspective in 1966, a crisis was undoubtedly at China's doorstep: the US was massively invading Vietnam, and the largest communist party in the world not in power was being the victim of a literal genocide in Indonesia, with US support. (Why is "genocide" not used for ideological groups but it is for religious groups? A religion is an ideology, certainly much more so than it is a *géno*, the Greek word for race.)

Other than making political statements to a Party, which contained many cadres who were only concerned about increasing their profits, he had only one other recourse – popular opinion.

That was all preamble. This brings me to that great and but bewildering story:

'Crossing the great river': to seize the moment you have to first understand the meaning

In the retelling of Fairbank:

"In the second phase of the Cultural Revolution from August 1966 to January 1967 Chairman Mao was a great showman. The dutiful Liu Shaoqi, already doomed for destruction, was orchestrating the anti-revisionist movement among the party faithful. In July 1966 the Chinese public was electrified to learn that Mao had come north, pausing on the way to swim across the Yangzi. Since rural Chinese generally could not swim and few adventurers had ever tried the Yangzi this was like the news that Queen Elizabeth II had swum the Channel. He was obviously a paragon of athleticism capable of superhuman feats. (Photos showing his head on top of the water suggest Mao did not use a crawl, side stroke, backstroke, or breaststroke but swam in his own fashion standing upright in – not on – the water. He was clocked at an unusually fast speed.)

Hilarious! And written with maximum effort for humour, too! What the heck was Mao doing?! Those inscrutable Chinese – we'll never figure them out! Mao was just being Mao – a capricious tyrant – but that one takes the cake! Elizabeth II swimming the Channel, LOL – good show!

It's too bad that Fairbank – perhaps the biggest molder of American thought on China for decades – had no idea why such a move *"electrified"* China. Fairbanks implies that Mao's demonstration was pure self-aggrandisement in the most Western-individualist, election campaigning of fashions: "I am so superhuman that I can crush all dissent – just watch me doggy-paddle over the Yangzi."

Too bad that makes no sense at all. It is totally intellectually unsatisfying. It also implies that Mao had become a stereotypical mad monarch, for which there is no such evidence.

Time and again Mao's swim is reported by Westerners as being loaded with symbolism for the Chinese people, but I have never seen the symbolism actually explained. That is too bad, because what this story does prove is just how close Mao was with the public and how he spoke their language; why the public adored him (still do and always will); and why he was such a People-trusting, People-liberating democrat.

Beyond political 'theater' & into the realm of political religiosity

This was the meaning Fairbank and many Westerners have missed, but which many of the People of China did not:

The ethical book of the Chinese is the *I Ching*, the Book of Changes, which is the world's oldest book in the world for a reason: it can be foolishly used as a divination tool – just as opening the Koran to a random page is used to "give advice" to some Muslims – but the *I Ching* is truly a master guidebook of social conduct, as well as human & Heaven-based morality.

Briefly, the *I Ching* examines 64 ethical, personal and social concepts, conditions and states. One meditates at length on a range of concepts – "Mutual Influence", "Bringing Together", "Darkness", "Proceeding Humbly", "Not Yet Fulfilled", etc. – and the book discusses their true meaning, how they progress in stages and how they interrelate with other concepts. Indeed, the interrelatedness of this first-ever binary system reaches a sort of "Social String Theory" level of unity, and with social morality & divine guidance omnipresent (though not Abrahamic, of course). By studying the *I Ching* one can see how, when and why these 64 ethical concepts / opportunities are appropriate (or not), and also get instruction on how they are likely to change – change being the only constant in this mortal world.

In this book is occasionally a phrase: "*Favorable to cross great rivers*".

When the *I Ching* reads that it is "*Favorable to cross great rivers*", that means it is the right time to dare the greatest of undertakings. Indeed, this phrase reflects the maximum amount of good and luck possible – it's the best possible news one could get from the book, and means Heaven above and Earth below could not look upon you or your plans more favorably.

I Ching judgments can be negative, neutral, slightly favorable, etc. So, conversely, if it reads "*Not favorable to cross great rivers*", it means – stop what you are doing and don't try it.

But nothing is better than *"Favorable to cross great rivers"*. It means something akin to: take courage, Heaven smiles upon you, you are just, you are in tune with ethics, in tune with the Tao (a Chinese concept very similar to the Holy Spirit), in tune with humanity and nature, etc.

So for Mao to literally cross the great river in July 1966 was to emphatically and physically tell all the Chinese People: "Join me in daring this great undertaking of the Cultural Revolution. Cross the great river now – in real life."

When one is thus able to look at Mao's swim through the eyes of a Chinese person and can fully understand the cultural context, as well as the historical/political context... then we finally see how it could have *"electrified"* China: For the Chinese, it is truly as if he had re-enacted a scene from the Bible.

The only way I could compare it for Iranians is thusly: In order to defend Iran's sovereign right to a nuclear energy program, Supreme Leader Khamenei travels to Karbala, Iraq...and has a boxing match with Mike Tyson. If you don't understand this... please don't pretend to tell me that you know Iran, our religion, and our culture. I'm sure Iranian readers are smirking, not because of Khamenei's advanced age and the absurdity of such a fight, but because they know exactly what I mean: This would be a reenactment of the glorious and assured annihilation – thus the martyrdom – of Imam Hussain, which inspires Shia as much as the suffering of Jesus does for Christians (even more in 2018, I would say, as the annual multi-million pilgrimages to Karbala show...and which Western media certainly does not want to show).

To explain it to the French: In order to demand the reversal of Brexit, neoliberal Macron goes to Rouen and fields media questions as he's tied to a stake.

For the Americans: acquiescing to Russophobia, Trump invites Putin over for diplomatic talks, but then personally captains a ship across the Potomac to surprisingly capture the Russian leader, like George Washington.

Did Mao know what he was doing?

As the son of a rich farmer he went to

school, where he was undoubtedly instructed in the Chinese classics, as education was centered around them. Mao also knew that other educated people were similarly instructed in the *I Ching*. The only question, which I cannot definitely answer, as I have never been embedded in Chinese popular culture, is: how likely is it that the average person was familiar with the sayings of the Chinese classics and the *I Ching*?

I think we can say with confidence: "At least somewhat familiar". Grow up in the West and you will be familiar with Biblical sayings even if you aren't Christian. Grow up in Iran and you will know all about Imams Ali and Hussain because they are so admired.

It is universally reported that the swim somehow galvanised the nation, and I doubt it was the view of an old man doing the doggy-paddle. In a perpetual question in semiotics: why this, and not that? I.e., why not climb a mountain to "electrify" the people, or chop down a cherry tree, or save a lamb? You certainly can't argue with the results – we can only try to explain them.

And yet Fairbank – the China scholar best known to the US public and academia alike – clearly had no idea of what Mao was doing, what it represented, and why it was inspirational. This means that Fairbank clearly had not even read the *I Ching*, perhaps the single most important foundation of Chinese culture, despite being Harvard University's first-ever China "scholar". That is a recipe for terrible scholarship, terrible teaching and ignorant-but-arrogant students.

It is a scholarship which is typical of the West, and which was debunked in its Islamic World-version so gloriously by Edward Said's *Orientalism*. It is scholars who don't go to foreign lands to learn and respect the local culture, but to proselytise their own ideas and to return with juicy, marketable stories, which confirm the standard stereotypes, almost as if they had never been there at all. Just as those who used to be called "Oriental scholars" never read *The Koran*, I highly doubt that Fairbank's knowledge of China extended beyond the superficial and beyond what was useful for him as an American.

So there is little wonder, to one who

understands the cultural significance, why China erupted in delirious, sweet, modern – and violent – revolution against reactionary forces shortly after the swim. *The swim was Mao's obviously successful attempt to get the People inspired*, and to reassure the People that (some of) their leadership was on their side, and on the side of preserving the popular revolution the nation worked so hard and for so many decades to install.

There are other facts and anecdotes of history to relate which defend Mao – his portrait is all over private areas in China for a reason - but I chose this one because it illustrates how Fairbank and the Westerners who have studied for China, and have given us our "wisdom" of Mao's alleged tyranny, actually have very little comprehension of the Chinese soul.

Their scholarship thus primarily exists not to defend objective ideas like "truth" or "respect", but to defend their own ideas. Such scholarship does not truly seek to understand the amazing qualities of other cultures, and are genuine only in their reactionary anti-socialism. And yet these are the people who inform today's students, journalists and citizenry in the West?

But a new type of Western scholar, such as Jeff J. Brown, wades unapologetically into the tidal wave of Western disapproval to deliver a history, which is actually sympathetic to Chinese people. I have tried to do the same, but obviously from an outsider's perspective, with all the advantages and drawbacks such a position obviously entails. Unlike Brown, establishment scholars on China are not trying at all to learn from, to understand, or to defend the Chinese people – they are trying to conquer it culturally. If that fails – then to conquer it militarily.

I could have continued giving more and more facts and statistics to prove that Mao's tenure greatly benefitted the average person – how long do you have? – because there are so very many. Thankfully, unlike when I was growing up, they are now actually available on the internet for all to find. They do not make it past publishing house or mainstream newsroom editors, but they are available, at least.

Instead of using statistics, I thought

this anecdote showed just how pathetically lost, how uninterested, how much lack of soul the people informing the West on China really have had. It is very similar to people who try to explain a religion without actually living that religion – its data can be related, but not its soul.

To prove my objectivity: A Chinese person is better qualified to verify the relationship between Mao's swim and the *I Ching*...but what if they haven't read the Chinese classics?

This hypothesis thus remains for the Chinese to verify... but I say the circumstantial evidence is weighty: just because I have not seen this hypothesis elsewhere, that only confirms that very few people have read the Chinese classics, and analysed them in a political sense, and written about that analysis in a Western language.

Fairbank obviously did not do this, even though it was his charge to do exactly that.

Rehabilitating Mao is unlikely - barring a change in sympathy in the West

John Lennon had it right in *Revolution* by The Beatles: *"If you go carrying pictures of Chairman Mao / you ain't gonna make it with anyone, anyhow"*.

Why? Because few people in the 1960s in the West were truly political (excepting African-Americans). Obviously nearly none were dedicated revolutionaries because the West had zero revolutions during this era. They looked to minstrels like The Beatles to lead a revolution – but the song *Revolution* is clearly designed to appropriate the word away from the political sphere: the lyrics are not just apolitical but 100% anti-politics.

Many in the 1960s sure postured like revolutionaries, though. My impression is that their main goal was to *"make it"* with the opposite sex, and that is really not something revolutionary in human history....

The irony is that if Lennon understood Mao – if Lennon had grasped the goal of the Cultural Revolution – he would have seen that Mao's 1960s anti-establishment, anti-corrupt "middle aged / old people" views, and his slogans like "It Is Right To Rebel", were incredibly rock and roll!

Politically, the fault is not with Mao, but with Lennon. Lennon is a typical Western political & spiritual nihilist, after all. In his song *God*, Lennon says he believes in nothing, including the I *Ching*, even listing it before *The Bible*. He also doesn't believe in people, ideas or methods: he only believes in himself. "*I believe in me/ Yoko and me/ and that's reality*".

So Lennon believed in individualism and his romantic love – that's nice...for him.

Lennon concludes *God* by opining that "*the dream is over*" – and that he, "*was the dream weaver*". The literal meaning for Lennon, the '60s icon, seems clear – or perhaps he was giving us a Hindu-inspired "life is a dream" idea. Lennon finishes by saying that, in 1970, "*You just have to carry on / the dream is over*". This reminds us today of the slogan "Keep calm and carry on" which swept England doing the 2009 financial crisis, a paean to their willfully-blind conservatism which will not countenance even the idea of discussing the idea of changing the status quo no matter how devastating the crisis.

What's sure is that, culturally, Lennon led the way for the West, and in 1970 he presaged their descent into total individualism & nihilism instead of maintaining his own cultural revolution.

So when it comes to Lennon and Mao: who is the man of the People, the social revolutionary and the ethicist, and who is merely another self-centred ego-freak? Who is the man of social change, and who is the status quo man urging everyone not to even bother trying? The answer is clear, and it is certainly the opposite of the West's mainstream belief.

Indeed, who would have thought that drug-using minstrels would ultimately get bored by worldly, wonkish, societal issues...? Maybe the West can next turn to a heroin-using jazz drummer for advice on urban planning models....

If you want to hear some raw guitar and a great singing voice, one may turn to

Lennon; but for Westerners to seriously turn to him for political guidance?

Should we defend Mao?

No, it will make us look uncool, and the John Lennons of the world will call us "squares".

The bad news is: you are certainly a square if you have bought this book and read this far!

Seriously: Yes, we should, mainly to humbly acknowledge the superior judgment of the Chinese people. The Chinese People defend Mao, and that should be enough for leftists worldwide. It is arrogance which refuses to defer to the judgment of locals, because unless you deeply know their culture, language, history, have lived there extensively, etc., it is pure arrogance to pass judgment on their key cultural matters. That is why I openly admitted the limitations of my interpretations of Chinese popular culture regarding my "Mao swim & *I Ching*" hypothesis. Popular approval is a nearly infallible judge, no? Castro, Khomeini, Ho Chi Minh, Sankara, Mao – all are universally loved in their home countries. Pol Pot, for example, is a leftist leader who is not revered by Cambodians so it's not as if all leftists are loved (Pol Pot was a rabid xenophobe, and thus not a true leftist).

Therefore, we must defend Mao, because we must defend the judgment of the Chinese people - to do otherwise is to claim that more than 1 billion people are incapable of thinking clearly. If 50 million Elvis fans can't be wrong, how can 1 billion Mao fans?

I think that Fairbank, even if he actually did talk to average Chinese people about Mao, was never willing to honestly report their opinion. Brown, however, has talked to "thousands" of Chinese people over his decades living there. He says that they criticise aspects of the Communist Party:

"But through it all, I can safely say that about 98% of the Chinese I've talked to like Mao and what he did for China. His image adorns taxicabs, like an amulet of St. Christopher, to ward off accidents. He is on walls of privately owned offices, businesses, restaurants – these are private, not government. They are citizens who have

127

decided to show their admiration for the man, on their own. He's everywhere. How can this be in the face of relentless demonization by Western media, educators, historians and politicians?"

People will say: it's because the Chinese government blocks the truth about Mao – oh, if only they could hear our pure Western voices!

Such a response, again, inaccurately and arrogantly implies that the West knows Chinese history and culture better than the Chinese themselves – the Chinese People *were there*, after all. The government has openly stated that Mao was "70% right and 30% wrong", so it's not as if there is an all-dominating, state-sponsored cult of personality, either.

Beyond respecting obviously better-informed local opinion – a point which most treat as secondary – I almost refuse to have the "Mao was evil" conversation for more than 15 seconds. I only give 15 seconds because I was raised to be polite....

To equivocate Mao with a tyrant like Hitler or a would-be Japanese emperor is to equivocate two opponents – it's inherently absurd. To claim Mao was as bad as Japanese fascist or American capitalist is also to equivocate groups with sharply different belief systems and goals. To claim Mao is worse or as bad as American, French or English leaders, who terminated millions while Mao tried to defend those millions from these foreign invasions, is absurd.

All of the claims that "Mao was evil" are based on historical nihilism and a complete disregard of the facts: In 1978, two years after Mao's died, China's Gini coefficient (the most commonly used measurement of inequality) was a sparkling 0.16. The lowest score is currently 0.25 (Finland). It's fair to say that Mao's single most-important goal was to create an equal society: he succeeded better than almost anyone, ever.

So I'm done with that one, and quickly. It's just too bad the other camp has no facts but overwhelming numbers....

Mighty Mao was never the West's to take away, and he'll never leave

The West's discussion of Mao – along with the Great Leap Forward's famine and the Cultural Revolution – is based on ignorance, arrogance and the political nihilism of failed "revolutionaries" and hardened reactionaries.

To repeat, for hard statistics about the socio-economic improvement for the average Chinese person during Mao's stewardship (and not just since Deng's reforms) you can buy Brown's book. Brown explains how Mao overcome a blockade worse than Iran's to produce massive growth with equality – Mao clearly had his cake and ate it too...and with his fellow citizens!

But, as cynical Lennon shows, it was always difficult for the West to grasp the moral, ethical, nation-inspiring and nation-building revolution Mao personified: they took two very different paths. What is so typically Western is that they insist on pulling China onto their toll road, instead of being content to live and let live in mutual peace.

Lennon famously said that Elvis died when he joined the army, but that's not true: Elvis died when he joined Hollywood after his discharge, and was no longer a great musician but just another phony actor. When did Lennon die as a revolutionary? The good news is that he didn't...at least not completely: Lennon sang *"But when you talk about destruction, don't you know that you can count me out"* on the single version of *Revolution*, but his political soul was back in the right place on the album version, where he sang *"count me in"*. It's not support for Maoism - it may even still be politically nihilist - but let's give Lennon a break as he was martyred and could not clarify his position.

No one is going to say Lennon did not succeed wildly in his chosen field, but how long can the judgment of Fairbank and other top Western "scholars" endure when we can so easily prove how they did not respect or understand Chinese culture? Even though it is fundamental for understanding China, nobody cares about Confucianism in the West – all you will hear about is its yin, feminine & passive counterpart – Daoism. Plenty of Daoism books in the local Western bookstore, for sure – how many on Confucianism? I guess yang, masculine, creative, dynamic, propagating Confucianism doesn't go well with acid trips, or high-intensity pharmaceutical drugs?

I'm not surprised that Communist Party is back to promoting Confucianism – the *I Ching* is not banned in China – and I'm not surprised they prefer it over Daoism, which says, "Cross the great river? What for? What river? Is this thing on?"

(Clearly I'm an even worse scholar of Daoism than I am of Confucianism.)

Nor am I amazed that the Western media views Mao as "100% wrong": The West has been an imperialist, extremist, racist culture for 500 years, and a rabidly anti-socialist one for more than 100 years.

But I am surprised that Western leftists don't defend Mao even 30%. Their main problem is: they have not bought books like Brown's...because books like Brown's simply did not exist until very, very recently. Prior to the fall of the Berlin Wall, a book like Brown's would have gotten you jailed in the West, or worse. A book like Dongping Han's would have never been translated into English. The internet is changing all this, and that cannot be stopped – only slowed.

And no apologies if my picture of Chairman Mao ain't gonna make it with anyone, anyhow. You know it's gonna be... alright.

For China, at least.

5

The Cultural Revolution's solving of the urban-rural divide

*I*f there is one thing the election of Donald Trump showed the United States it's that there is an enormous urban-rural divide.

That's not true at all...

The US "discovered" this exact same problem following the elections of Bill Clinton and George W. Bush: rural voters found Clinton immoral, urban voters found Bush immoral – open support for either president made one immoral. Both were vilified as totally unacceptable leaders by either the city mice or the country mice. Both presidents were atrociously immoral and unacceptable modern leaders, of course.

However, 2018's unprecedented animosity (although the animosity towards Bill and "Dubya" were both called "unprecedented", which perhaps only proves that the US keeps escalating in their tension and violence) towards Trump only shows that undeserved self-righteousness has temporarily swung back to the urban sector. But the reality is that anger is simply what American mice do: they are angry, and they think that the venting of anger equals power, when most everyone else knows such lack of restraint equals the opposite. But this anger is a phenomenon endemic across today's West: the French public is aggressive, culturally chauvinistic *and* incredibly rude; England trails only the US in an assumed sense of superiority; Canadians are the kings of passive-aggressive behaviour, and the list goes on.

The capitalist-imperialist West's enormous political dysfunctions, faulty presumptions and roads they refuse to take... I cannot offer a remedy to all these things, but this chapter does discuss *real solutions* to their unbridged urban-rural divide. Due to the mass urban migrations of the 20th century, this divide is felt more acutely by rural inhabitants, while being a latent ache in urban dwellers, but it is clearly a cultural and political dysfunction which must be immediately remedied...and which China has already has.

There can be no remedy to this divide if we don't acknowledge how timeless and universal it is: the urban-rural dichotomy is as fundamental to human society as male-female, old-young, home life-social life, science-faith, etc. Creating a satisfying cultural synthesis is thus a difficult & never-completed but still urgently necessary undertaking.

China had a big leg up in this particular dichotomy thanks to the Confucian hierarchy of gentry/scholar-farmer-tradesperson-merchant (-soldier), but the West gives no such value to the rural producer of everyone's food. The West has advantages in other cultural dichotomies - true meaning of "globalism" means giving China their due and learning from them.

At some point, the West's urbanites (often effete, annoying, condescending and ultimately intolerant) are going to have to realise, accept and appreciate the timeless fact that this dichotomy *is indeed valid and sensible*, because different values are needed to thrive in rural settings than in urban areas; therefore, rural values must be as equally promoted as urban values in the overall national culture, in stark contrast to the current policy of denigration and exclusion. A problem is that urbanites insist that their values are at the crest of the wave...but very often it is a wave of mere fashion. Another problem is that urbanites view their wave as an all-erasing tsunami, rather than just one moderate-sized wave on one side of the island. But there is little doubt that the values of rural areas are more enduring because they are more adapted to nature, which certainly runs a longer timespan than those of powerful cities and their cultures.

Just as men and women must get

along despite their natural differences, so must urban and rural – here are some definite answers.

How do we solve the urban-rural divide? Change the culture

I have a very simple solution for the West: have their version of the Chinese Cultural Revolution, which had the bridging of this urban-rural divide as one of its main tenets.

Of course, my idea will be met (unfairly) with shock and horror, because Western propaganda is that the Cultural Revolution was an unceasing cavalcade of horrors and injustices. Chapter 3 discussed the true, known and factual motivations, policies and results of the Cultural Revolution, which are ignored in the Western media in favor of tabloid, self-serving coverage. The dominant Western view of the Cultural Revolution is thus a reactionary and certainly prejudiced view - accept that and it makes it possible to *at least consider the need* for certain aspects of China's Cultural Revolution in your country.

Iran doesn't need a Cultural Revolution - as mentioned, they had the only other official one in world history. There were talks of a second one with the election of the first Basiji president, Mahmoud Ahmadinejad, but it never materialised. The Basij is an organisation which is totally unknown in the West, but whose only parallel is the Chinese Communist Party. The Basij also serves as a sort of guarantee of permanent and cultural revolution in Iran - Iran has clearly studied and learned from China, unlike the West.

China, as I detailed in Chapter 1, is largely geographically unsuited for farming and yet they have always held the global championship belt for "World's Best Farmers". As I mentioned with the Confucian hierarchy, their esteem for rural life made it easier for China to solve this divide, and also made it only natural that Maoism was the first socialist philosophy to place the farmer on a perfectly equal basis with the modern industrial worker. In short, just as the West in 2018 so fervently believes its problems are caused by the racist hicks of rural areas, Maoism so fervently believed the opposite.

The question we should be asking is: Why did Mao believe in the cultural worth of rural values?

Well, he spent years in the countryside, so he knew how they lived. Familiarity breeds (some) contempt (in the long run), but total ignorance surely cannot breed understanding. He was not in an ivory tower, nor stuck in a bohemian part of the city, nor surrounded by like-minded factory workers. Instead of making the country come to him, Mao actually went to the country (and made a rather Long March around it, too).

But how many urbanites in the West have lived in the countryside for more than a weekend, and not in the sequestered experience of a childhood summer camp?

I'm an urbanite, and prior to 21 years old I could count the number of times I had seen a cow on one hand. But then I lived exclusively on a farm for more than 1.5 years. To say that it was an eye-opening, humbling experience is an understatement. I quickly perceived how shallow my worldview truly was, having been totally limited to urban areas. I realised how very rich is the life of the rural people whom urban culture told me to disparage and feel superior to. I often compare the experience to someone who lived in strict gender segregation until the age of 21: how full and rich is life alongside our other gender, and how empty without it? Male-female, yin-yang, city-country – all of these represent two opposites of perfectly equal, yet different, powers. My worldview, my understanding, my compassion, and my soul were all irrevocably, and quite necessarily, improved by the experience. But in my discussions with Western urbanites I have rarely come across people who claim to have had genuine experiences in both urban and rural settings.

So when the Communist Party sent everyone from mild reactionaries to city-kid students to the countryside during the Cultural Revolution of the 1960s, I am personally certain that it was most often a positive thing, and I am not surprised that it is reported that the era is fondly remembered in rural areas. The Party knew it would be reforming and supremely enlightening because it would increase the scope of one's understanding of the world, affirm the experiences of other people and thus increase one's love of humanity and of life itself. Rural areas are good - case closed!

The West's problem becomes even more profound when one realises that the West's leaders have not had these types of necessary, rounding and lengthy rural experiences...and that China's leaders have: China's President Xi spent seven years in the poor countryside during the Cultural Revolution. Xi lived with lice & hard rural labor, with nights spent reading to illiterate farmers (which he credits for making reading his greatest passion). That's even though his father was the Party bigwig who created the first Free Economic Zones across from Hong Kong! This is another aspect of the Cultural Revolution - your degrees, your money, your status and your parents do not matter in a modern society. Emmanuel Macron, in contrast, spent time at Goldman Sachs. Dubya Bush spent time owning and running the Texas Rangers baseball team (and trading Sammy Sosa).

Hillary spent time looking down on the people of Little Rock, Arkansas and callously planning her success / her opponent du jour's downfall.

My political enlightenment on the rural-urban issue came through talking with others – not just watching the corn come in and go out. Without the rural friends I made, and without their patience in correcting my uppity, uniformed city slicker bullplop...I would be a far, far worse person today, and certainly a far, far worse journalist.

What we need to realize is that the only remedy for urban elites is indeed to get them out into the country long-term - and vice versa, of course - enlightenment cannot be a short-term project. China's Cultural Revolution should start appearing not so drastic, but as the only solution to a universal cultural problem.

New, simple policies to make this change in the West are obvious: Civil service programs and public propaganda campaigns to support them. Compulsory service in the armed forces provides another way for people to see how the other half of their country lives. Of course, this will take the ever-so-incredibly-valuable time away from the neo-aristocracy's suburban high schoolers and the after-school programs they need so desperately to get into capitalist-restricted higher education; the discipline, humility and slogging work such a program requires and creates will also conflict with the "hustler" capitalist mentality promoted on every urban street corner and in every media. But what is a society which does not promote sacrifice for the greater good and not just the personal good? Answer: a purely capitalist one.

The propaganda battle will require just as big a cultural change: Phrases such as "flyover country" will have to be seen as what they are – signs of reactionary thought, whereas they are instead bizarrely seen as some sort of signifier of leftism/liberalism. The old rural values – and I don't need to list them because they're largely the same as the seasons – must be promoted with at least equal vigor as the modern urban values of detached alienation, disregard for home life and "be cool, cool, cool" even at 65 years old. Clearly, something like a "cultural revolution" would be required to make this long-term and lasting change in the West. Hmm, I wish somebody had thought of that earlier...

The bottom line is: I just don't see how the urban-rural divide can be crossed *without crossing over*? The mass migration of rural to urban during the 20th century makes it clear which side has to make the move.

How do we solve the urban-rural divide? Change the land

This section takes an unexpected tack – let's not first worry about rural land ownership, but urban land ownership.

A reason why there is so little ability for urbanites to spend serious time in the country learning about the countryside of life is because they are under such constant financial pressure... to pay higher rent. The cost of living, and especially housing, is far greater in urban areas, of course.

A fascinating cross-cultural study was issued in 2017, which found that Paris and London had the highest rates of social psychosis. What I found of great interest was that owning your home – or not – was found to be the single biggest indicator of mental and emotional stability. Research published in the prestigious Journal of the American Medical Association found, *"the strongest area-level predictor of high rates of psychotic disorders was a low rate of owner-occupied housing"*.

It is quite logical: When a person is constantly worried about being able to pay the rent, or when the rent can be raised without warning or limits, a person cannot feel themselves to be truly stable. In societies where only the rich can afford housing without concerns, then the myriad small neighbourhoods, which compose a country, necessarily become full of unstable people:

*"People in areas that are socially deprived (*i.e. not rich*) may have more social stresses, which could predict psychosis incidence, as suggested by other studies,"* said a researcher. *"An alternative explanation could be that owner-occupied housing is an indicator of social stability and cohesiveness, relating to stronger support networks."*

The researcher is right on both counts: "land poverty" (i.e., not having a stable, long-term home) is a stress, which creates psychosis, be it mild or severe. And non-"*owner occupied housing*" (i.e., forcing to hand over 1/3rd to 1/2 of our paychecks every month to a rich, two-home owning landlord (which was likely only inherited from his parents) means that people are forced to move a lot, have shorter ties to the community, and get into debt. The land issue means that capitalist communities thus have inherently reduced "*social stability and cohesiveness*".

And also, the lack of a stable home shoots the whole "civil service program" in the foot: What is the point of making a multi-year cultural revolution if people have no place to return to where they can implement and share what they have learned?

This study was the first of its kind in 25 years, and I highly doubt it was geared towards proving the necessity of socialist housing for urbanites - but it clearly does. China did not need such a study to prove what is just common sense – that housing laws must massively favor renters and not landlords, and that is at the very least.

So pity poor Western millennials: In a stunning and completely foreign notion to anyone born after 1975 in the West, 70% of Chinese people aged 19-37 own their own home, according to a study by British bank HSBC. Number 2 in the study is Mexico, at 46%, with the US at just 35%. Just 69% of French millennials say they plan to buy a home in the next 5 years, the highest in the study. The French are noted for their pessimism, but in this instance I'm surprised they are so optimistic: have you seen Paris real estate prices?! I have no plans to do so, and I'm 40 years old – who is going to pay for it / force housing prices lower? In 2018 the second global real estate bubble has produced record prices in Paris.

Western culture thus has to actually try and spin this lack of stability as some sort of positive: Western young people are supposed to be considered lucky for being "free, flexible & unencumbered" and other such nonsense. In reality they have no job security, no stable home, massive debt, are untethered to society and thus suffer from endemic alienation.

"Bread, peace, land" can be translated to "Bread, peace, a decent apartment" in modern times.

But it's not only China and not only Maoism which has solved this issue, proven by their 90% home ownership rate overall. 80% of Cubans own their own home and thus pay no rent or mortgage. Can you guess the common denominator here?

How do we solve the rural-urban divide? Central economic planning

The socialist way is "central control but not central management". The capitalist way is "local control and no management (except for market forces).

History repeatedly proves that this puts rural areas at a fundamental economic disadvantage *in toto*: There is simply no way to safeguard the rural half without central economic planning – they will always be left behind because helping hillbillies will never turn an immediate profit even though it certainly seems like it should. Except for politically advanced places like Cuba (where fuel shortages provoked by the international blockade required the mass creation of urban food gardens), food, the ultimate currency, is produced in the country... but the money flows to the cities via their middlemen, distributors, commodity exchanges and banks. And it stays there, at least in capitalism. This is the only reason rural societies wind up being perennially poorer than urban societies - they are certainly pulling their societal weight!

While this fact should be well-known already, the structural causes of the natural exploitation inherent in the rural-urban divide are supplied in multiple eras of Chinese history. Whether he realized it or not, the right-wing Fairbank makes the case for central planning as the only solution to end the urban-rural economic divide:

"Deng and his successors realized that in order to move to the market, it was necessary to decentralize and to reduce the concentration of political and economic power in the central government; but they did not foresee the extent to which such an economic and political decentralization

would result in a decrease in the flow of taxes to the center. This diminished the reach of the party state authority and fostered an informal federalism. In the short run, decentralization helps economic development by allowing more tax revenue to stay in the local areas to stimulate growth. But in the long run, as occurred in the late Qing Dynasty, it leads to a relative decline of central government revenues and thus decreasing expenditures on education, health, and infrastructure, eventually undermining economic growth, especially in the countryside."

Whether it is in Qing-era feudalism or modern neoliberalism, without economic central planning to redistribute revenue money will flow in a largely one-way direction from country to city *in the long run*, creating an economic rural-urban divide.

Fairbank continues, and Deng-era capitalist failures will sound very 21st century neoliberal:

"As revenue declined, the government shifted much of the responsibility for investment to the local governments and enterprises. But while they were prepared

to invest in economic projects, local governments were less ready to invest in education and health... Likewise, with the abolition of the communes which had provided the funds for healthcare, education, and infrastructure development, particularly public irrigation networks, rural communities could no longer finance their own public activities. Evidence indicates that rural health, education, and public works gradually deteriorated in the 1990s."

And this is exactly where the EU and US find themselves today: without central planning in order to fund unprofitable rural infrastructure... it simply never gets constructed, and thus the urban-rural divide is never bridged. Socialism differs from capitalism in that the government exists in large part to provide needed services, and not to turn a profit. Crazy right-wing Americans say that unprofitable rural towns deserve to die and that rural citizens don't need opportunity and equality but simply need to *"get a U-Haul"* and move somewhere else, to quote the phrase published in the *National Review* American neoconservative magazine, which caused a minor media storm in 2016 for its incredibly reactionary stance. *"The truth about these dysfunctional, downscale communities is that they deserve to die,"* wrote the author. Well... that is not a humane, intelligent, realistic or culturally-sustainable solution; that's the cultural-cleansing of half the country, and it justifiably increases the anger of rural residents towards the urbanites who propose such a "solution".

Furthermore, in the modern and universal context of increased absentee landlordism – the 19th century phenomenon of landlords moving to the city, thus divorcing themselves from rural society, and thus drastically increasing rural exploitation (this is discussed in greater detail in the next chapter) – only the government can play the role needed to fully protect rural societies from urban exploitation. The urban-rural divide may be timeless, but what goes ignored is that it has been exacerbated in the past two centuries by industrialism and modern capitalism, and that it is being manipulated even further during the era of digital high finance.

The irony is that the great Western breadbaskets – the Midwest for the US and France for the EU – already do have major subsidies to protect their farmers, but the subsides are mainly for their farming corporations and not small farmers. Central planning is thus not at all new to the West, but socialist (non-corporation centered) central planning certainly is.

The urban-rural divide is not existential - it can be addressed

The Western view of the urban-rural divide seems to be: "take no prisoners in this cultural war". That's a problem, because I don't know how we could eliminate one without the eliminating the other.

Wait – what?

"What" indeed, my rigid Western friend! The unity of yin-yang, male-female, urban-rural and other "opposites" is only irreconcilable in Western contexts – they are viewed natural, desirable and absolutely necessary complements in Chinese-influenced societies. Until

Westerners learn to respect the "other" – races, religions, cultures, national regions, etc. – their unbalanced self-centeredness can only continue to manifest itself violently.

In the globalist era of "the modern person is a proud citizen of no nation", perhaps whether one identifies as "urban" or "rural" is actually the 21st century's most fundamental "nation"?

This modern intolerance between urban and rural is not a major problem for everyone, however: as Fidel said, a divided society is an ideal society for imperialists. And what else is "identity politics", so revered in the West, but a way to divide people based on differences instead of uniting them based on shared traits (such as class)? Of course, identity politics is a tool against socialism, and obviously reactionary, divisive, inherently isolating & alienating, guaranteed to provoke anger & narcissism, etc.

Certainly, making these fundamental shifts – in national popular culture for humility towards rural areas, resolving the land issue, and economic planning to defend rural areas (and not just multinational farming corporations) – requires nothing less than a cultural revolution. I am not expecting one tomorrow in the West, but nor do I see a solution without one.

China provides the example...but China's example was more than a bit violent – if the West could study and learn from the Cultural Revolution, perhaps theirs could be less bloody?

But too many perceive China's Cultural Revolution as boring as watching the cows come home – they need to find the revolutionary poetry in both. If ever there was a universal dream, its to see your bullying grade school teacher wearing the dunce cap - China's Cultural Revolution is obviously inherently fascinating! This is why - unlike the demonisation of Mao or tabloid-ready famine stories are far more popular than the Cultural Revolution - the West is right to largely ignore it altogether.

The main step, I believe, is to realize that *there is no getting over the rural-urban divide* – it is too fundamental to human existence – there is only synthesizing and celebrating it. China is way, way, way further along on this issue than the West.

Maybe you don't like my solutions to the West's rural-urban divide? At least I am providing an attempt at a mutually-beneficial cultural synthesis based on respectful cooperation, rather than fomenting intolerance. Turn on your TV – how many Westerners are promoting that with their rural areas?

6
Once China got off drugs: the link between opium and 'liberal warlord' Macron

*T*he link between Chinese opium money, monarchies, and rich Western families (Astor, Forbes, Kerry, Delano, Roosevelt, etc.) is already well-known, though it's not publicised enough in the mainstream media. What is even less publicised is how in 2018 the drug trade creates a country – Colombia, Afghanistan, even the United States, etc. – which becomes so socially, culturally, financially and politically dysfunctional that the current neoliberal ideal of being being anti-big government starts to appear...rather sensible. And thus, neoliberalism wins converts among the 99% who should be promoting socialism, with its insistence on significant government control to promote their needs over those of the 1%.

The era 1841-1949 is called the "Century of Humiliation" by the Chinese, but Western histories call it the "Treaty Century", the treaty primarily being the forcing in of Indian opium. Therefore, a far more accurate term would be the "Drug Treaty Century"... but that wouldn't be effective Western capitalist propaganda, would it?

What's interesting about China's opium wars is how very modern they are – China's forced drugging was not a millennium ago, but during the birth and installation of our modern political era. Therefore, aside from birthing modern fortunes, drugs also helped to birth modern ideologies.

In a sense this chapter is a bit of a

digression, but it is in many ways the most practical: We can quite clearly chart how in 19th century China drug money fostered a *nouveaux riche* which in three generations (a generation being roughly 33 years) became the key driving force behind the armed obstruction of China's socialist and democratic reforms after World War I. As I will show, this Chinese group is ideologically equivalent to "modern conservatives."

This chapter goes into much greater detail sociological detail, but here's a brief recap:

We can all agree that China during that century – whatever you may term it – was exactly like a country today in *Françafrique*, or one of the banana republics dominated by the US: it was an unpopular regime controlling a divided country; foreigners controlled the key areas (the capital, the ports & railroads, the mines and other sources of natural resources); petty tyrants were recruited in order to control the local population in "flyover country"; the governing ideology was Western ideals mixed heartily with the practice of amoral *realpolitik* and pitched at an absolute cultural war with the local historical ethical system.

If this sounds undesirable... then you are in agreement with the constantly-rebelling Chinese of this era.

But if we dispense with the racist, chauvinistic notion that the Chinese somehow deserved all that because they were "incapable" of "modernising" due to "backwards" or "unscientific" ideas (feel free to insert your own preferred nonsense here), then we are freed up to realise: Drugs were the grease which powered this society-undoing machine.

It's interesting to recall that drug money was not a factor in the 1917 Russian Revolution – so when they toppled their imperial monarchy, socialism was immediately installed. China was not so lucky. This chapter examines the political consequences of this historical difference, and it concludes that the "Drug Treaty Century" created a new "drug lord bourgeoise" which created obstacles that required a much longer march to socialism than in Russia. But, more interestingly (I think) is how this chapter also shows that 19th century

China proves that the drug trade can create a social situation so dysfunctional that all governments appear inherently ineffective, producing a situation where everyone in the 1% and the 99% is led to believe that the ideals of big-government democratic socialism are only a recipe for guaranteed social incompetence.

This drug-fuelled incompetence occurred in China a century ago, and it produced the clear ideological forerunner of neoliberalism; this drug-fuelled incompetence occurs in many nations today, and it produces modern neoliberalism.

But there's a reason they call it "dope", dope.

The drug trade: A simple Western recipe for nation-destroying

Drugs are not good, and we all know this. The ability of Westerners to get nearly 100 million Chinese people – 1 out of every 4 – on opium in the 19th century was...not good.

Understatements aside, is there any

product, which is more superbly capitalist than drugs? There is no regulation, competition is cutthroat without limitation, and the profit margins are in the hundreds of percent – it's better than arms dealing!

But it is no overstatement to say that it is profoundly shocking to list the macro-level, societally-destabilising conse-quences drugs had in 19th century China, and which occurred in just a single generation: Drug money increased the resources and thus the success of foreign warlords (foreign imperialists). Of course, they were the first ones to profit, as they were the "first movers" in the Chinese drug business. Drug funding allowed the English and French warlords in East Asia to occupy Beijing in 1860. They installed the totally ineffective Empress Dowager Cixi, who ruled for almost 50 years (1861-1908), and they "forced open" (invaded and occupied ports and railroad towns) China to "modernity".

Because drugs are so much more profitable than anything else, the drug trade also created the resources to pay for establishing overly-powerful regional

Chinese leaders (warlords), who reduced the power of the central government. These warlords, to protect the power they took from the central authority, created their own armies and professionalized the military class, elevating it as never before in Chinese history.

Opium is still trade, even if it is opium, and it necessarily requires mid-level merchants: this meant the rise of a bourgeois gentry as never before in China. Merchants and soldiers composed the bottom two rungs on their classical Confucian hierarchy (and soldiers are not even officially granted the status of the bottom rung). This is the exact inverse of capitalist Western society, and we see how Westerners upended Chinese culture upon their very first contact.

Drugs also exacerbated the pernicious rural-urban divide: Increased money for "traders" meant the ability to buy more land and become even richer, which meant the ability to move to the cities and run your affairs from far away via a local bully, which dissolved the ancient, much-needed bond between landlord and tenant. This may have been the deepest socio-economic effect.

Drugs provide cheap spirituality, and dangerous religious cults sprouted up. Christianity was introduced, but for every one Chinese person converted forty more became addicted to opium (not just consumers). Hardly a moral proselytisation to an Abrahamic faith...

Concurrent with all of this, and also amazingly clear, is how drugs fuelled not just poor governance, but ultimately the anti-government sentiment, which is now a hallmark of today's neoliberal form of capitalism. If the government "sucks", to use the parlance of our times, then getting rid of it as much as possible is smart, right? China's government certainly started to really suck....

By the 1860s the drug trade allowed for a new tax on this "trade", but this new source of income for the central government meant they no longer were pressured to rely on receiving taxes in return for providing good governance or adequate public services, thus deteriorating the quality of governance in China. The foreign-provoked drug trade essentially rewarded the central power with money for *not governing* (ignoring laws against drugs, ignoring the decreasing health, stability and quality of life of their citizens, etc.).

The rise of drug money created the resources for traders and the gentry to bribe officials at all levels, further reducing the central government's ability to govern properly. And that's even among those pubic servants who actually tried: For example, when the central government attempted in 1884 to fix the tax system it was quickly abandoned. The only reason for such poor policy is corrupt, inept government – corruption techniques clearly permitted the interests of the new local drug lord bourgeois to win out.

The trade was also so lucrative it provided local "warlords" with resources to provide their own government services, making them appear superior to the central government. Thus "big (centralised) government" begins to be fairly disparaged as being staffed by lazy, incompetent and / or immoral people – echoing today's complaints – even though these new local "leaders" made their money off drugs, instead of real work. This repeated weakening of the imperial prestige due to this bad governance encouraged more support for local warlords, who are the ultimate capitalist supporters. This further eroded the national / central authority and thus their ability to govern well.

All these combined social catastrophes culminated in multiple rebellions and civil war: the "Taiping Rebellion" (1851-1864) was a multinational affair, which the English and French took advantage of to prop up their puppet, and which gutted Chinese society as significantly as the American Civil War and over roughly the same time period. These rebellions also caused the government to respond by militarising the countryside for the first time since the Qin era (221-206 BC). The war effort also caused the rise of new taxes on peasants, which never endear one to the government.

That's quite a few kicks in the teeth to the idea of good & centralised governance, no?

To recap: The West's (drug) "Treaty Century" was – in the span of just one generation – able to 1) totally discredit the central government, 2) discredit all government, 3) discredit the longstanding cultural and religious authorities, 4) foster the rise of self-interested, unpatriotic, extremely violent local governments, 5) create new classes of super-landed rich, who turned into an out-of-touch, absentee, uncaring urban elite, 6) foster corruption at all levels, 7) create spiritual chaos, 8) create political-cultural chaos and elitism, because who can have faith in the democratic ideal of the self-governing abilities of one's neighbours when 1 out of every 4 of them is on drugs? 9) actually create situations of open rebellion against the government, 10) create situations of the societally-draining need for armed resistance to invading powers.

And things only got worse in the two coming generations!

The link between drugs and capitalism, and thus anti-democracy, is clearly illuminated in modern Chinese history: Imperialism, drugs and bad governance clearly have a synergistic effect, like the sky-high cancer rates of people who worked with asbestos and also smoked.

Indeed, the history of socialist-inspired countries which have true wars on drugs – China, Iran, Cuba, etc. – illuminate this link, and also explain why their zero tolerance efforts are so strong and their punishments so harsh. I imagine that the Dutch would not have been so content to be drug-happy if a foreign power had been the one controlling its influence in the Netherlands?

Again, this clear cause-and-effect between Western-backed drug schemes and the end of non-Western society as we know it is obviously not limited to just China, but has been replicated in countless societies in 2018:

One may not support the ideals of the Taliban, for example, but what chance did they have to improve Afghan society when the US invaded and made opium production higher than ever? Indeed, many Afghans undoubtedly say that life under the Taliban was much better than living in the state created by US imperialism. Opium has, once again, been used to totally create a dysfunctional, divided society, which doesn't know what is up or down, just as it did in China pre-1949.

By Generation 2, the taint of drug money is gone & cultural revolution is underway

The various effects of drug money – quite logically – totally reduced support for any government by making them appear incompetent... which they were.

By the 1890s China was so weakened that the Japanese invaded, and China lost the Sino-Japanese War. Payments required to fund this failed war caused the monarchy to become heavily indebted to the West.

In 1900 the Boxer Rebellion – against foreigners and arrogant Christian missionaries, but unlike the Taiping Rebellion now allied with the imperial dynasty (rallying cry: "Support the Qing, destroy the foreign!") – saw China become effectively split: the rich south allied with the foreigners against the rebellious north. Opium had made the southern "capital" Shanghai the new vice capital of the world and also the home of China's new "trade" bourgeoisie (we know of mainly which product). Effectively an entire continent was split and not just a country - balkanisation under Western auspices, and to the detriment of the local 99%, as usual.

Clearly, by just the 2nd generation of the "Drug Treaty Century" China had totally fallen apart politically, morally and culturally.

The drive to remodel China's political culture began in this 2nd generation. We must strive to put ourselves in the shoes of the Chinese back in that era: Just as the ideals of socialism are being heavily discussed in Europe and Russia, there is one generation already in adulthood and another one growing up with the idea of government as a completely-negative force. Monarchy is on the way out, but socialist ideals are being heavily discredited from the get-go, with resources being stored up to fight against it: "Socialism and this new guy Karl Marx?! Government by and for these drug-addled clowns?! No thanks – I'll get, and keep, mine by any means necessary."

This 2nd generation thus sees China

changing from a "China with Chinese characteristics" to a "China with West European (bourgeois) characteristics" – it's a cultural revolution, and one far more truly horrific than in the 1960s.

The new Chinese drug lord bourgeois were – being bourgeois – ultimately a class loyal only to themselves, their power and their money. They had unprecedented means to reshape classic Chinese culture in the Western bourgeois mould, and they did. This nouveaux riche class will sound quite modern:

They worked with foreigners for personal gain at the expense of the nation's 99%. They claimed to be "philanthropists" who supported charities with unpaid taxes that should have gone the central authority. However, these charities did not capably replace the reduced central government services, of course. They denigrated the state bureaucracy as incapable. They claimed to be "activists" who promoted modernity, but were mere individualists promoting their own interests. They remade society's most important instructional force – education.

In 1901 major school reforms started, adopting the Japanese system which – unlike Vietnam and Korea – was not strongly influenced by China's civil service test. (Japan is, in my mind, a Western country: "Western" is a culture, and Japan went over whole hog, as evidenced by their decades of imperialism – this did permit them to avoid getting the fast-drip China Drug Torture treatment.) The government examination system was unwanted by the new drug-money elite because it was meritocratic: its existence directly challenged the new concept of the "private school" (a foreign concept imported to China), which the 1% use today to maintain their dominance.

Indeed, the privatisation of schools – the loss of state control – serves to transfer control of schooling to the 1%, and schools henceforth exist to indoctrinate a new technocratic class, and one which is loyal to their privileged class and not their own People or their own nation. What is the biggest anti-union drive in Anglophone countries today? The drive to privatise schools: if capitalists are successful, one of the biggest remaining unions will be no more; a huge percentage of the government will also disappear, which necessarily reduces the government's overall domestic influence.

So we should not be surprised to see how Fairbank celebrates the end of the Chinese civil service tests:

"Alas, it was soon found that students would continue to aim mainly at the old examinations as a more prestigious and much cheaper route of advancements, bypassing the difficult modern curriculum and greater cost of the modern schools. There was nothing for it but to abolish the classical examinations entirely in 1905. This great turning point stopped production of the degree-holding elite, the gentry class. The old order was losing its intellectual foundation and therefore its philosophical cohesion... The neo-Confucian synthesis was no longer valid, yet nothing to replace it was as yet in sight."

Of course, the old gentry class had mostly earned their status through aristocratic and reactionary nonsense, but at least some of their merit and some of their class members joined via passing the civil service exams; the new gentry class only earned their status via the drug trade. "*The neo-Confucian synthesis was no longer valid*" only to foreign invaders and drug barons. Fairbank, being unsympathetic towards Chinese culture, and certainly unwilling to allow it to stand strongly and in opposition to Western dominance, celebrates the death of thousands of years of native culture because he wants to replace it with neoliberal capitalism.

Revolutions in learning are fine, but not when they are not focused for the benefit of foreign capitalists and the local bourgeoisie, whether China's drug lords or modern Brussels' technocrats. Indeed, then these changes are not "revolutions in learning", but reactionary, stultifying and impoverishing changes. Ultimately, these schools were remembered for producing the "warlord generation" of 1916-27: certainly, this represents the true apex of China's Westernisation.

What's hugely important to realise is that the 99% of the second generation of the "Drug Treaty Century" *certainly did not agree* that nascent neoliberalism had brought local benefits. The people hated this switch to "local governance", and thus they had major rebellions, of which I only mentioned the two biggest, as is common. Fairbank admits this, but doesn't really care, as he is a neoliberal capitalist-imperialist:

"'Local self-government,' despite its happy resonance in the minds of Western advocates of democracy, had its own rather different meaning for the Chinese common people. The term in reality usually designated a managerial agency of the local elites, which they used to secure their villagers' taxes to support modern improvements. Road building, setting up modern schools, and paying for police were improvements desired by the modernizing elite, but paying higher taxes to secure them increased the villagers' burden faster than it benefited them. There were many peasant protests against 'reform'."

Sadly, by 1908 the drug profit-fuelled gentry had too much money, too much land and too much power: the Empress declared a constitutional system, with 0.4% of the population (all men) allowed to vote in a bourgeois system. This 0.4% were not just drug dealers, but European-apers in every way – they were the selfish bourgeois merchants and militarists (whether in open or secret) which Western society is based on. The monarchy – gutted by foreign debt from the Boxer Rebellion (Against Foreigners And Arrogant Christians), unable to restore power usurped by the provinces, out-spent by the new bourgeois class and unable to create a unified army – abdicated in 1912 and was replaced by the Chinese Republic.

Bourgeois constitutionalism in the context of a monarchy is – history, and also today's newspaper, repeatedly proves – a pact between the monarchy / aristocracy & the bourgeois elite against the 99%. However, even Fairbank admitted the 99% wanted no part of this change, because the Chinese imperial system – where a Heavenly Mandate rested upon demonstrably good governance and not mere bloodlines, like in Europe – was arguably superior to Western Europe's "modern" democracy despite being imperial, because China ostensibly switched from a pact between the monarchy and the 99% for a pact among just the 1% themselves. For nations without popular, socialist-inspired revolutions a monarchy-1% pact, or a pact to self-deify the 1% and boot out the monarchy, is where history effectively ends and their present is found. This is the mass majority of the world's nations!

But for Western academics like Fairbank, the clear tragedy which was these first two generations of the "Drug Treaty Century" could never be lain at the feet of obvious collusion between a new, Chinese, free trade-loving, drug lord upper-class and their Western warlord allies. Instead it was the natural result of the inherent stupidities of Chinese culture and, that old standby, the "*passive*" character of the average Chinese person (which, along with "*docility*", Fairbank also employed as a politically-scientific explanation to explain both the Great Leap's famine and the Cultural Revolution):

"*These inadequacies of the old regime in administration and finance were deeply rooted in Chinese custom, political values, and social structure. It became apparent that the Qing government had been superficial, passive, and indeed parasitic for too long. It could not become modern."*

Fairbank – as is custom in the United States – may be against monarchical rule, but he is definitely not against aristocratic-technocratic-1% rule....

Clearly, by the birth of the third generation China's drug-fuelled failures had destroyed seemingly everything, and of course the bourgeois are all-too happy to pick up (and keep) the pieces.

Early Chinese drug barons were truly just 'modern conservatives'

Just as Westerners inaccurately call it the "Treaty Century", it is also inaccurate to call this 3rd generation the "Warlord Era", as is common: these warlords were not tribal savages, as the name implies, but instead the supporters of West European (bourgeois) democracy and modern conservatism. And yet despite the crystal-clear similarities, I have never read of an early 20th century Western small town or big city politician demoted to a "warlord", much less even Hitler or Mussolini?

"Warlord Era" is thus a racist term which allows Western people to fancifully indulge in allusions to Ghengis Khan which only they find witty; crucially, it also reveals a racist mindset when viewing China which helps them to deny that China could ever be "modern" like the West. "Warlord Era" allows Westerners to picture the Chinese as an unchangeable Yellow Horde, when they were really just plain-old modern conservatives. This is a common tactic of not just Fairbank but all pre-Politically Correct Western academia: repeatedly dehumanising non-Whites and making it appear unthinkable that modern Westerners can feel kinship with modern non-Whites, in the pre-current and less sophisticated form of today's "identity politics" (instead of "class politics").

But it was indeed the case that we are talking about obviously-recognisable modern conservatives: these "warlords" also had anti-socialism as their *raison d'être*, and were indeed the Chinese fascist Brownshirt-type of leaders who were everywhere in Europe and America in the 1920s and 1930s. The fascist supporters of Chiang Kai-Shek were known as the Blue Shirts.

China's fascists, like their European

peers, were capitalists but they had the virtue of at least being "nationalist capitalists"; "neoliberal capitalists", however, have no nation whatsoever. This is why neoliberalism – who are currently dominant, probably because they are so unsentimental and ruthless – deride any modern nationalistic capitalist movement as "fascist", "populism", "Trumpism", etc. In 1930's China nobody was crazily saying "I'm proud to have no country" just yet, but the times do change quicker than we all think....

I take this quote here from Fairbank to describe the ideology of this group of neo-bourgeois, which he applied to the first generation but which obviously not only holds true but had become even more entrenched by China's third generation:

"From the perspective of modern times they were conservatives. Their eventual alienation from the effete Manchu ruling house would be based on the cultural nationalism of Chinese patriots determined to preserve not only their country but also their own social leadership and domination."

If one insists that Fairbank would not

have used that quote to describe the 3rd generation, that's fine with me: I'll happily agree that modern Western conservatism is equal to what passed for modern in 1840s China. Modern Western conservatives are that outdated! But, clearly, the quote holds true into the 1940s.

China's drug lord bourgeois were indeed all in favor of the harsh repression of modern conservatism's main targets - moments for socialism, organised labor and feminism. Make no mistake: These social trends had obviously reached China too, and no more so than in Shanghai, where Chiang massacred communists and made the Kuomintang undoubtedly modern fascists / conservatives.

"At Shanghai Chinese merchants soon stood opposed to the new and leftist labor movement. In this stance they had foreign support. In reflecting many years later on his raising funds at Shanghai for crushing the labor movement Chen Guangfu stated the aim had been to topple militarism, the warlords, and support a modern government."

Fairbank here quotes and elevates

Chen Guangfu (known in the West as K.P. Chen), who was one of Shanghai's most powerful US-allied entrepreneurs and high financiers. The *"foreign support"* for this pro-fascist, anti-socialist supporter was obviously the US and other West European nations. Chen was truly a modern, small-government, no-nation neoliberal, and thus Fairbank is trying to exonerate his funding of the massive massacres of human beings for the crime of being leftist. This is modern conservatism, of course.

However, repressing *"the new and leftist labor movement"* – which certainly included feminist, racial-equality and other socialist-inspired popular movements – can never be considered "modern". China's pre-communist government is only a "modern government" to West European (bourgeois) neoliberals like Fairbank, who are clearly the same ideologically as Chinese warlords (and from anywhere between 1839 to 1949 – your choice).

The monarchy-free drug lord gentry and their foreign supporters would have been quite happy if the Republic of China still existed today instead of the People's

Republic of China, of course.

Emmanuel Macron the 'liberal warlord', tool of drug barons (and spouse of one, too?)

Somewhat thankfully, President Yuan dissolved parliament in 1913, setting off civil war. Or to use another racist Western term employed by the likes of Fairbank: "*civil warlordism*".

Certainly the United States battle between the industrialised North and the Confederacy's aristocrats was a far more barbaric "*civil warlordism*" – one side was defending slavery, after all. But "*civil warlordism*" is only reserved for China - not only because of the ruthless effectiveness of the ancient Mongols, but because Mao and other Chinese socialist leaders were nothing but opportunistic warlords to the likes of Fairbank, even though they fought to end China's bondage.

But China's less than decade-long experience with bourgeois constitutionalism before rejecting this West European invention thus almost perfectly parallels the Russian experience.

A major difference exists: Russia was fortunate enough to have a drastically revolutionary concept to implement – socialism – whereas China was not as much at the crest of this wave of progress; China was further from the geographic centre of this movement in an era of limited communication abilities. And, again, 25% percent of Russia was also not using drugs.

But make no mistake – Yuan, in collaboration with the drug lord gentry, ended the Chinese Republic specifically in order to forestall socialist-inspired changes:

"Having initiated the 1911 Revolution that ended the imperial check on their power, the provincial elite (which did not exist in the imperial era, and which only rose to power recently during the Drug Treaty Era) *resumed their stance for stability and so 'gave a pivotal support in 1913,' says Esherick* (Joseph Esherick, one of Fairbank's own proteges), *for Yuan's assumption of dictatorial powers. Their instinct was to save China from the chaos that they feared further change would*

create. In this way conservatism thwarted any social revolution."

That is exactly what modern conservatives do in 2018 – use dictatorial powers to thwart social progress.

We clearly see the antecedents of today's "liberal strongman" like French President Emmanuel Macron, who is using rule by executive decree – i.e., dictatorial powers – to deconstruct socialist policies and programs which existed before he came into office. Therefore, "liberal warlord" should be the term used by those historians who come from the opposite side of the political spectrum of Fairbank in order to describe modern France.

Macron is indeed equivalent to a Chinese/Taiwanese warlord: Not only is he waging imperialist foreign wars in Africa and the Middle East, but he is waging domestic war against his own people (having made nearly all the extraordinary powers of France's 2-year state of emergency common police practice). as well as repeatedly and profoundly undermining the prestige, services and reach of France's central government.

Scientists, and many women, might even say he is also a true drug baron: he married into a chocolate empire!

But the line is clear: Anglophone golden-boy and neoliberal darling Macron is the clear ideological inheritor of these drug baron bourgeois. While the West may have a short memory and an actually-short history, the year 1849, to a Chinese person (and an Iranian one) was not that long ago – this line is straight and now proven.

(I won't countenance that Macron is actually pro-government because he pushes for more EU government, and for multiple reasons: The "more government" does not at all equal an increase in true democracy given the fundamentally undemocratic and neoliberal structure of the Eurozone and the obvious anti-democratic decisions of the European Union; I think he knows they have no chance of even getting approved; these are many of the same ideas which the French 1% have been pushing Germany for since after World War II; and this pro-government stance is not more defining of Macron than his obvious disregard for democracy, his disregard for the opinion of the 99% and his disregard for the importance of a socialist safety net.)

Both Macron and China's drug lord gentry want a bourgeois ruling class, which lives apart from a continually-impoverished 99%, and which has no problem denying modern democratic changes and suppressing popular rebellions: "Modern conservatives" and "liberal warlordism" indeed....

Show me a country awash in drugs, and I'll show you a capitalist-imperialist nation

Unlike a typical drug crash, we can still finish on a high note!

It is impressive how quickly this bourgeois Western republic fell: the Chinese people quickly saw that socialism was needed but – unfortunately – that required a long civil war provoked by modern conservatives and liberal warlords.

Fairbank, a modern conservative himself, must have known that he was on the wrong side: he even relates how Mao knew the problems caused by West European, bourgeois, "modern", "multi-party" democracy, all of which are similar today. Fairbank cites Mao in 1926:

"Peasants are oppressed, he said, by (1) heavy rents, half or more of the crop, (2) high interest rates, between 36% and 84% a year, (3) heavy local taxes, (4) exploitation of farm labor, and (5) the land owners cooperation with the warlords and corrupt officials to exploit the peasantry in every way possible. Behind this whole system laid the cooperation of the imperialists, who sought to maintain order for profitable trade in China."

Ya can't say Mao didn't see things clearly... We see how applicable this is to modern times (indeed, our elderly were living in this recent era!):

Just replace high taxation with "continuously low wages / purchasing power" and the effect is the same; interest-induced debt slavery remains unchanged; in a Europe which is seeing the rich Germans, French and Dutch cannibalise the weaker Greece, Ireland, Portugal and others, it's clear that Western warlords have merely ended their previous White

Power solidarity and have started imperialising their own race.

Just as Chinese opium created riches in places far from China, so it impoverished political thought in both faraway lands and faraway times as well. The EU, as I have proven in many articles and which was already-well known, is a series of structures which are defined by being anti-democratic, anti-socialist and unrepentantly neoliberal. And in drug trade nations, they are pushing in this negative direction as well. Compare the differences between Columbia and Venezuela: One nation is the leader of Latin neoliberalism and the biggest tool of Washington in the region, the other is the leader of South American socialism – despite being neighbours and being in regular contact, their peoples and cultures couldn't be more different. Ideology counts - one remains proudly stuck in the mid-19th century, the other is being invented daily.

Indeed, I am certain that if an outside imperialist force were to be applied to the paradigm of Western societies (which are militarily impregnable in 2018), we would certainly see how neoliberalism would immediately descend into chaotic *"civil warlordism"* – because that is what happened in modern China. And it was only socialism that was able to defeat that corrupt, elitist, capitalist system.

The reason for this may be because the visions of earthly paradise in capitalist and socialist societies are very, very different. The capitalist view is clearly quite drug-addled: their goal is to retire rich at 40, live in sensual pleasure, free from societal constraints, and to have the ability to rule their tiny empires like petty dictators.

Modern socialism's vision is superbly expressed in China's lovely, enchanting phrase a "moderately prosperous society". I love that modest ambition for materialism! And it so obviously implies ethical self-restraint in order to promote equality. The phrase was used as a set of key political slogans by current Chinese President Xi Jinping, but it goes back to Confucian times.

What is far more important than preserving the right for an individual to completely satiate their materialist ambitions is to have the universal stability required to do the good works necessary to always preserve an ethical, harmonious society.

If you disagree with that: what are you... on drugs?

7
Prefer the 1% or the Party? Or, Why China wins

*T*he Chinese communists kicked out the Japanese, then the Europeans, helped hold off the American neo-imperialists at Korea and then again in Vietnam, provided spectacular economic growth during all that time, ended rampant drug abuse, forbid ethnic quarrelling, and is the economic envy of the world in 2018.

Maybe you don't want to live there, but you certainly wish your country were doing as well for itself as China is. Every Third-Worlder would agree with that in a nanosecond, and only a French-style superiority / inferiority complex could cause a Westerner to deny it.

How did we get here? Divine intervention? Cultural superiority? The dumb luck of an electron's random path?

Somebody is running political-economic policy, and the West European (bourgeois) system and socialist-inspired Chinese system answers quite clearly who has been doing better since the Developing World gained (often nominal) independence in the 1960s. And if you've read this far you know all that already, so I'll spare you the preambles and get right down to the nitty gritty.

So who's your Daddy?

Everybody's got a vanguard party. Democracy is not perfect (only God is), but this does not mean there are not varying degrees of perfection which we can analyse and attain.

In the West, your modern-era vanguard – after decades of money-grubbing, back-stabbing, standing on daddy's rich shoulders, and exploiting those who work for them – is the economic 1%. To add journalistic balance: they also got to be the vanguard via the admirable ethical business practices of Jeff Bezos and Bill Gates, the genius of people like Warren Buffett to support the growth of private & socially-abusive monopolies, and the incredible skills of being phony in public by actors like Ronald Reagan. These are whom have been chosen in the West – via both informal and formal democratic consensus – as their vanguard party.

According to Fairbank, China has always been culturally predisposed towards rejecting that type of a vanguard:

"Once the literati who set the tone of ruling class opinion became convinced that the dynasty had lost its moral claim to the throne, little could save it. This is a factor in Chinese politics today."

If I said that Chinese literati ran China I'd be called "romantic", but that's the view from a pair of Western eyes, which can usually only imagine the army, money, or an only-negative, reactionary clergy to be the the deciding factor in politics.

However, we can say that there certainly was a literati in charge in Revolutionary War-era America – it was bourgeois and slave-owning, but they often talked the right anti-imperialist talk

197

and walked it, too. But nobody can say that about America's leadership today: I don't know what the 9th century Chinese theatre equivalent of the Reagan-and-monkey-starring movie *Bedtime for Bonzo* was, but I don't think the lead actor got as high on China's political ladder.

In France, every politician must write at least one book, but...c'mon – they are imperialists, cultural chauvinists and fake-leftists, or somehow all three at the same time quite often. However, at least France is not American, eh?

China may or may not have a "literati" in charge today, but you certainly cannot possibly rise in the Communist Party without being literate in modern political and economic theory. Call me "Confucian", but the best way to lead is by example – so what example does their current vanguard party give us?

Just how good is China's economic planning? There's a reason we aren't told.

I'm going to put the juicier section – China's economic planning – ahead of an "as painless as possible" quick recap of the Chinese political structures which permit such a juicy economic policy.

The reality is that people are right to fear rule by the Party – it's radically new. In human history it has been the 1%, 99% of the time. Even in aboriginal societies, how often were women and the disabled allowed to make major decisions? Therefore, we have almost no data to rely on regarding what happens when an 99%-inspired Party rules.

Common sense tells us that public opinion can't rule 100% of the time....but should it only rule just once every 4 years? The scientific method tells us that data and testing are important – we should use them in politics and not just the chemistry lab, no?

A great thing about Brown's book is that he gives us plenty of evidence which leaves no doubt that China's system uses data better than any other government to find out what the People think: it is a People's *democratic* dictatorship, after all, and they absolutely cannot have democracy without compiling data on what the people say they need, want and generally opine on important subjects. The modern reality is that China compiles and actually draws from this "People's data" hugely impressively. It is also a reality that Western parliaments care very little about public opinion on seemingly all policy making, and certainly Western executive branches are not constrained by it either, nor is the European Union or Eurogroup (which runs the Eurozone).

The disparity between China's reality and image is startling - a "5 year plan" is portrayed as pure dictatorship, but here's how it's actually compiled, per Brown:

"These five-year plans are not done in a vacuum. A vast hierarchy of information speeds up from village committees to county, district, provincial and then national levels. These statistics are based on surveys and polls of the masses. The Communist Party of China is one of the largest polling organizations in the world, obsessively interested in what citizens think about, the good, the bad and the ugly, from garbage services, to medical care, to the ability to buy food or a car.

Computers have made a huge improvement in collecting and analyzing all this information but still thousands of statisticians, actuaries, database experts and technicians who studied at university in urban, rural, agricultural, environmental and economic planning, hundreds of thousands of collective work hours to interpret and analyze this soon army of data statistics and information....Needless to say, for a continent-sized country with over 1 billion citizens, it takes hundreds of thousands of people involved to develop each five-year plan."

It is not *"needless to say"*, however, because such facts about China's governmental and economic process are never uttered in the West. They must fear that we would be contaminated by such democratic common sense. "China is an unfeeling totalitarian system...and they're capitalist, too. End of story!!!"

This is where new China scholarship by Brown should revolutionise the conceptions of China for those who are honest; Brown has lived there for nearly two decades and is involved in normal, everyday life as an active immigrant-citizen, as his book repeatedly demonstrates. He relates how he knows that polls of all types, and of all demographics, are taking place because he sees constant flyers for them in his regular-class neighborhood. Fairbank will always be "Harvard's first China scholar", but he can never outclass Brown on "new", living China scholarship, though he probably does outclass Brown on old, outdated, scholarship of centuries-dead Chinese.

In the West public opinion is polled just one time: during election time, and then is totally ignored. French President Emmanuel Macron and others pride themselves on not listening to public opinion once reaching office, and he is steadfastly implementing whatever the hell he wants. During election campaigns modern candidates like Hillary Clinton bend any way the latest poll is blowing. Among the People of the West there is abundant proof of support for leftist policies, and certainly majority support for many socialist-inspired policies, but they are totally ignored because they are unable to play a role in the West's money-centered, 1%-created and supported, bourgeois, individualistic political process.

Not so, socialist China…

"Compared to Western countries, what is amazing is the lack of serious influence that China's private sector has on the process of developing each five-year plan and budget. The idea of having thousands of lobby and special interest groups, let's be honest, with hundreds of millions of dollars and euros in hand to essentially buy legislation for their direct benefit, is alien to Chinese governance.

Do various, aforementioned government entities contact the offices of Jack Ma (Alibaba), Robin Li (Baidu), Wang Jianlin (Dalian Wanda Group), and others among China's elite business world? Of course. But the idea that any of these CEOs or their companies go to the state planning commission or National People's Congress, with checkbook in hand, to write and buy their own laws, which is standard practice in Eurangloland (European Union, NATO plus Australia, New Zealand and Israel), is unthinkable in Communist China. Their wishes and suggestions are surely known by everyone concerned, but they are trumped by Baba Beijing's overriding priority of maintaining social stability, called wending *in Chinese, and keeping the Heavenly Mandate for the long term. And these Chinese movers and shakers in the business world are in total agreement. No wending is very bad for business, unless you sell arms and weapons, and almost all of these in China are state-owned."*

Brown clearly does not have red-colored glasses about the increased access of China's 1%, but he demonstrates that the real project of modern socialism is to not to destroy capitalism 100% but to limit it and harness it for the benefit of the 99%.

"Suppose Baba Beijing declared a serious funding issue or the masses began to turn on their superrich 1% class, which is now looked upon with a certain amount of national pride? The National People's Congress might feel compelled to pass a law requiring all fortunes over $1 billion dollars to pay a 10% or 25% wealth tax to the state treasury. China's 1% may grumble and complain, but the checkbooks would necessarily be whipped out. They know the only reason they have accumulated the wealth they possess is due to the Communist Party of China's strategic, long-term, five-,

and now essentially 10-year economic plans, and all the well-thought out strategies, subsidies, targeted tax cuts, etc., that were bestowed upon them. There is no sense of thankfulness on the part of Western capitalists for what their governments do for them, because they now they own the process in the first place. How can you be thankful for something which you already consider yours by right?"

The key here is that, when it comes to economic planning, socialist-inspired countries have huge leverage to force their economic direction in a way which guarantees – *guarantees* – to be pointed in a way which is *at least primarily intended* to help the 99%. Nobody can guarantee economic growth, perhaps, but central planning is a far, far more secure system than trickle-down economics and the boom-bust cycle of capitalism.

Undoubtedly, the above quote demonstrates how China is no "individually planned" economy like Macron's France or the Eurogroup for the Eurozone, both of which are clear betrayals of the ideals of Western democracy. The Western capitalist model certainly pales in ethical comparison with socialist democracy, which insists on some equality instead of unrestrained individualist rights.

"*In the West, the politicians and policymakers owe their allegiance and existence to the one percent, with their vast sums of money. In China its one percent owes its allegiance, existence and vast sums of money to the Communist Party of China, its politicians and policymakers.*"

That is socialism – it is the opposite of individualism; greatly undermining *rampant* individualism – not all individualism – is the only way to socialism. It would be nice to reach the ideal of no private property and total equality among citizens – that is communism – but, to paraphrase Fidel: we must change today *that which can* be changed.

The Chinese Communist Party has limited rampant individualism in order to insist on the unity and brotherhood of all peoples by cutting off at the knees the false idea of the self-made man. Truly, anywhere, everywhere, and at all times in history people have made fortunes thanks to help – subsidies, protectionist policies, corruption, favourable loans, etc. We are all connected, whether mighty yang CEOs or soft-yet-enduring housewife yins. This acknowledgement – inherent in socialism – is why the Chinese are winning, economically.

Governments DO change – all systems are NOT alike – China's system and practices are stunningly effective, obviously, and stunningly modern as well. But to get so stunningly stunning, there must be a legal foundation to promote and protect such stunningness.

There is a hugely important mistake many people commonly make: People in the past were younger, and thus stupider, while those who are living today are actually older, and thus are the repositories of more experiences, maturity and human intelligence. So why on earth would anyone think a country with a constitution 200 years younger (the US, written 1787) than China's (written 1982) is somehow "more modern"? The world was so much younger and stupider then - do we not all say the exact same thing about ourselves?

Part of the problem is the use of the phrase "the people's dictatorship" – whoever sired it, dictatorship is generally disagreeable to modern ears. However only the Western media uses this two-word phrase! It is truly disagreeable to Chinese ears, as well – the preamble of the Chinese constitution uses a very different term: "the people's *democratic dictatorship*". This is not a small nuance at all.

China is not really totally ruled by the Party: You never hear this in the West, but there are eight other political parties known as the "Democratic Front". As their name implies (democracy currently being more associated with personal freedom than equality, for some reason) they are more capitalist and personal freedom-oriented. Far from being a token, they account for some 30% of seats in the largest national legislative body or parliament – the National People's Congress.

Just as I always say Iran's PressTV is more diverse and open than Western media – because even though our editorial line is clear we have rabid pro-Zionist analysts all the time, whereas the West doesn't even have Arab analysts when they are talking about Palestine, (much less Palestinian analysts) – China's top legislature has far more ideological balance than the English-speaking world does. The 30% is not in charge – by law – but they are there, and they do make a difference. There is no such ideological political tolerance in the English-language world, where Hillary passes for a leftist; Corbyn is a very new phenomenon; Canada and Australia have totally lost their sense of self and are US-aping neoliberal (and I may not have written that 30 years ago). Continental Europe does not merit being lumped in with the "keep calm and carry on" Anglosphere... but not by much, as their non-mainstream / true leftist parties have dwindled greatly - the "Eastern Bloc" is a shell and being overpowered by the a rising far-right.

My overall point is: There IS ideological balance in China's top legislative body, but it is not a perfect balance NOR should it be. The West has 50-50 balance between (alleged) left and right regularly...and it produces total gridlock. Probably because it's a balance of "bad" and "worse", ideologically!

China also outdoes socialist Cuba in this area: In Cuba's brand-new parliament – just the 2nd female-majority parliament globally, and with 40% Black or Mestizo members – only 10% of members are not members of the Communist Party. I'm sure that's never reported in the West either…

But, socialist fanatic that I am repeatedly imagined to be, both China and Cuba (and Iran and Vietnam) have succeeded because they allow more ideological balance then they are given credit for. We socialist fanatics like to remember that those horrid souls called "the opposition" do have some valid ideas to implement…

Lobbies are not really democratic - China puts those pigs in a pen

Why should you have more influence just because you are rich and well-connected? You should not be able to "pay" for more free speech just because you have the money to do so. If this is considered a lamentable inevitability, then structures are needed to limit it, or simply eliminate it entirely.

That's why China has another national body, which is designed to formally harness an uncontrollable force in the West: special interest groups. Indeed, if you find any nonsensical legislation in the West – the root cause is always a lobby.

Thus, parallel to their parliament, China has the Chinese People's Political Consultative Conference, which contains all the different types of lobbies – private industry, farmers, youth, pensioners, etc. This body meets at the same time as China's Congress (Parliament), so they are democratically present at the key time and can do their best to influence opinion.

And I think I have been able to explain – quickly and without boring you – China's top legislative bodies and how they work. Clearly it is superior in conception, composition and practice to West European (bourgeois) democracy… and if you can just hang in there a tiny bit longer I can sum up China's modern advantages in the other two branches of government.

China had enough of warlords, but the West loves 'liberal warlord judges' like Macron

China also differs in the executive branch: in the West it is personified by Emmanuel Macron, the new "liberal (free market / non-racist) strongman". Macron rules by decree *even though* his Party has an absolute majority in Parliament! That's because the open debate of his far-right economic policies would inspire a lot of bad press. Truly, he's an emperor in the old Chinese mould... minus the conscience-pricking Heavenly Mandate, of course.

China's system, instead, spreads out the power of the executive branch in order to safeguard the control of the vanguard party – the Communist Party – which has been democratically installed by their 1949 popular revolution. This decentralisation of individual power to preserve the power of an entire Party is what socialism is all about: no more strongmen (and certainly not during non-wartime).

Thus the 300-member Central Committee (of the Communist Party) is the first step above the Congress, but the members are voted for by Congress. That is indirect election, and the US has this (the electoral college), as does France in a slightly less-worse system (500 mayors are required to sign your petition in order to be able to run for president). Cuba just elected Miguel Canel-Diaz and their Central Committee via the principle of indirect election. You can call the socialist system "not democratic", and the socialists can call the capitalist system "not democratic", and that will allow me to move on with this analysis...

The Central Committee elects the members of the Politburo, Military Commission (Party control over army) and General Secretary (leader of Politburo and the top post in China). The Politburo is often described as an "executive cabinet" but it's much more powerful: of course, in Western cabinets they all serve the will and at the consent of the king. Macron's cabinet has absolutely no real individual power; his predecessor François Hollande had four prime ministers in 5 years. There is no public debate within a cabinet and there is no public debate with the Politburo, but the latter's members are undoubtedly known to wield much more power than Western cabinet members. France's Prime Minister actually was known for having significant power in shaping domestic policy, historically, but Macron - child of the neoliberal era - has changed that drastically. If his proposed constitutional reforms pass, France's president will also have officially usurped the role of the prime minister.

Within the Politburo is the Politburo Standing Committee, which is chosen by Politburo members, and which is best described as similar to a Western cabinet, as it includes the president, premier and the nation's top 5 to 9 advisors.

To sum up: The Chinese People vote for Congress, and then you have these committed Party members winnowing themselves down democratically via three smaller rings. The key is: there is tremendous democratic discussion within these rings, though it is not in public. This is something which Western media either cannot or will not understand. But this is why most of the decisions are unanimous – consensus is agreed upon before a vote via discussion. Why on earth should public policy be a "winner take all" situation – China's solution is clearly more democratic because it actually produces more compromise. Brown goes into Chinese "face saving" as a reason for not publicly filibustering like a blowhard, and it makes sense, but Cuba's negotiations are private as well because, again, *it actually produces compromise.* Yes, odd gadflies cannot pore over every word, but the proof is in the pudding of China and Cuba's long-term success amid decades of Western blockades.

Back down at the local level, China has the inhabitants of one million villages vote by secret ballot for mayors and city councils. This is the exact same in the West. It differs above this in that China switches from direct to indirect representation after the municipal level: those directly elected at the municipal level vote for township, in turn for county, in turn for province, and then province votes for national assembly.

So we see the same principles of direct and indirect democracy are undoubtedly at play – as they are in Cuba, Iran, etc. – and are at play at different levels. But both principles are used and accepted in both the capitalist and socialist democratic systems.

The major difference is that decades of freedom-fighting and leadership caused the Chinese people to insist on a single vanguard party to oversee the country in order to preserve democracy, and not to hand it to one liberal strongman warlord. Iran is the same way: our vanguard party, which provided decades of freedom-fighting and leadership (which is the only way such a party can possibly have the credibility and influence needed to mobilise the masses) was the clergy.

To sum up this recap of the structure of Chinese socialist democracy – a quick note about the judicial branch: China's judicial history is longer than anyone's, and is pretty interestingly rendered by Brown. It had explicit civil and penal codes predating not just the Magna Carta but Jesus Christ; has an informal/communal justice system which is the same as the one currently being hailed as groundbreaking in Northern Syria / Rojava; and has notes of French and German civil law. Undoubtedly there are Muslim influences as well, given that many Khans were Muslim and were favoured by the Ming dynasty. This is an area which merits further scholarship, as it is certainly a mine which will yield plenty. It would also provide counter-illumination for self-understanding in many Muslim countries, because countries like Iran were controlled by the Mongols for quite a long era and thus have many "Chinese"-origin policies, though we may not know it.

The main difference between China and West in the judicial branch is quite simply: the judicial branch is explicitly under the leadership of the Communist Party – a group is the ultimate judge.

In places like the US and France: The ultimate judge is the president. State of emergency or not, they routinely subvert justice simply by claiming "terrorism". This is not new: before that it was by claiming "communism". Before that it was by claiming "White superiority".

So, from Chinese eyes, someone like Macron has made himself into a "liberal warlord judge" even more than previous French warlords!

There is another vital difference: In the West, the inhabitants are encouraged to believe a fiction that their judiciary is completely unaffected by politics, wealth, religion or ethnicity. The West also believes in Santa Claus, but that's mainly their children.

The same policy of: "A claim of objectivity is laughably unmodern, and also cannot be more important than our overall Party principles" applies to China's fourth estate – the press. The West also believes their press achieves objectivity, but that is not only among their children.

What have you done for me lately, or let me do?

German, French and English leaders have spent the last 150 years leading horrifically bloody battles against each other. Therefore, is it any wonder that the current European leadership – exemplified by the undemocratic, unaccountable, banker-dominated Eurogroup – is so reactionary, and so unable to provide the standard of living their people deserve? From a very well-supported perspective, Europe is perhaps only at the tail end, or perhaps even still in the midst, of a major era of warlordism.

This is probably why there are so many protests in the age of austerity in France. China thinks that's great, and surely encourages France's very cute, very comparatively *petite* efforts at modern democracy - as I mentioned the rate of public protest is less than half that of China. I also doubt that Chinese protests feature alcohol and proudly scatological protest signs so ubiquitously. Protests are good because they let a government know about urgent problems, which need to be resolved. These are problems, which have not been headed off beforehand, say, by... I don't know... public polling?

The US has essentially no protests, and the ones I have seen on Youtube were led by such an obviously-inexperienced citizenry that they were thwarted by two cops on bicycles.

Protests in Iran are far, far more

common than Westerners think. There is no way for Western media to cover every Iranian protest with the breathless anticipation of the fall of the Iranian Revolution over 10 days in December and January in 2018. Protests need permits, just like in France, and I'm not sure what if the US requires a permit or not before some 130-kilo once-a-month National Guard member gets to don $100,000 of equipment before stepping into his assault vehicle. Iran is not China, nor is it France, but it is also not Cuba.

Cuba, does not have any protests other than the "Ladies in White", female relatives of jailed dissidents. Like in Iran, religion is rallying point for political activity - their marches are based around Sunday Catholic mass. Cuba, being so close to the United States, simply can't afford to mess around – not with protests, not with the media, not with drugs, not with crime, not with corruption, not with focusing your meager tourist dollars on anything but food, housing, education and medical care (and that's for the medicines which are not part of the embargo). They have no oil, have a pack of rabidly capitalist

Scarfaces glaring at them from Miami, and yet are a helluva lot more successful societally than any non-socialist inspired government.

France, which is assumed to be so very, very socially successful, keeps putting tear gas in my eye. I am not crying tears of liberation, and I have narrowly avoided worse. They also have a delusion that one day of protest does anything to an uncaring government, and we can definitely say that "May '68, 50 years later" was a failure.

The excellent news is that the 1% has no chance against the Party...any Party

Brown reads the tale of the tape simply and perfectly:

"Xi commandeers a centrally-planned state-owned economy being guided by the Communist Party of China, all of whom are planning years and decades into the future, with a clear vision and solemn mission statement. Meanwhile, Obama has packs of rabid hyenas circling him, the spydom pack, the military pack, corporate pack, bankster

pack, not to mention the Zionist pack. Then he has to deal with a huge flock of vulture legislators on Capitol Hill, venal, fatted and corrupt to the core."

That is the 1% in a nation of any colour or of any religion, which is capitalist and "multi-party".

And if you believe THAT is superior to an enlightened vanguard Party working to enforce the People's will, then...your problem is structural; your blindness is cultural; your willful individualism is grating to me.

The idea that what Brown has failed to report is that: in China there is a 1% and Deep State-guided industrial-military-banking-media complex *on the exact same model* of the West is... absurd (and is political nihilism). But I can see why the West would think that: humans often project their own experiences onto others, as it is far easier than seeing others as individuals.

China does not have the burden of such a complex. Another reality is that the West's "rule by the 1%" is not burdened by any mandate of good governance or equality, either cultural or found in the structures of their 200-year old founding documents.

Furthermore, the idea that in the modern era of capitalism known as neoliberalism, the West's 1% has any solidarity *with even their own government* runs directly contrary to their vision of globalisation.

These last three points are all rather enormous issues, no? Well, it's not the Party's problem...

It is lazy stereotyping to say that China has this superior leadership because of the Confucian focus on correct, virtuous conduct of the ruler, for which there is nothing similar in the West. Islamic Socialist Iran certainly has this ideal omnipresent in their government - God watches. However, this idea denies Westerners the chance to see that China's socialism is both modern and open to all for adoption – it is not culturally predicated, but is a political choice.

Trump just pulled out of the JCPOA on Iran's nuclear energy program, but all he will do is cause short-term economic pain: Iran, like China, has a modern government which has 5-year plans and *can actually act* in the long term - they are ruled by the Party, as the 1% was kicked out in 1979. I hope Iranian officials are reading Brown's book and adopting certain Chinese strategies, of course, but Iran has a People's Democratic Dictatorship Under God, and I am truly comfortable with our long-term success (Inshallah). Anybody who loves socialism, Islamic or not, and the right of People to choose, should be pleased to hear that I and many Iranians actually feel secure in our future despite Trump's decision, which is clearly the same as the hyper-aggressive policies of Obama, the Bushes, Clinton and Reagan. In the short-term...well, the US making problems and killing people with blockades - there is nothing new about this, nor does this make Iran special, sadly.

All the West can do is threaten to invade – to repeat their warlordism – but I am not worried at all for places like China and Iran. They can never invade (much less hold) either of these two – they haven't even been able to invade far, far, far poorer Cuba! The reason for that is: all these countries are ruled by the Party, and not the 1%.

The inherent truth behind this reality is clear to any observer, and is the reason why Western media is so against any victory of socialism anywhere in the world. It is also why they have no choice but to try and falsely claim the credit for China's economic success even though the two have economic and political plans *which have tremendously few parallel structures*.

Once one becomes familiar with new, honest scholarship on China, such propaganda becomes laughable... and then one becomes rather envious!

You should be too. Certainly, any thinking person in 2018 begins formulating their response to the question posed by this chapter's title with: "Well I sure don't want the 1%..."

8

China's only danger - A 'Generation X' who thinks they aren't communist

When you have a world war, there is no question: We are all living in a postwar world. However, not all subsequent generations have been shaped the same. By debunking the standard view of the Cultural Revolution in chapter 3 we see that China's mid-1960s political revolution succeeded even though parallel cultural upheavals failed to produce the nearly-identically desired systemic changes across the West.

Because China was seemingly the only 1960s revolution which actually succeeded in rebooting their political system, we are faced with a question to which the Western postwar experience doesn't really apply: How will China's post-1960s generations develop, and then lead society?

We all know what followed the West's political failures of the 1960s:

Baby Boomers have proven to be totally incapable of taking the torch from their "Greatest Generation". The Clintons, Dubya Bush, Obama and Trump are synonymous with corruption, hypocrisy and stupidity, and both America's 99% and the rest of the world are unhappily living under their most inglorious reign.

That's not my opinion – just talk to any Westerner and they are totally dissatisfied with their systems, excepting only the tiny, isolated Nordic countries: Denmark has gone from Shakespeare's place where something was rotten and depressed to winner in the UN's annual World Happiness Report (2016). But the fall of the USSR has allowed the average Westerner to become duped into believing

TINA (There Is No Alternative), and are too underpaid and over-burdened to have time to be involved with political alternatives.

The children of Baby Boomers became known as "Generation X", who became disillusioned, navel-gazing and appallingly apathetic to all things political. This second generation clearly did not think much of their parents - in no uncertain terms they proclaimed that Baby Boomer political "glories" were just lying stories. They were right (excepting only African-Americans, who did not win anything close to what they wanted or deserved but did end Jim Crow). This 2nd generation refused to honor their parents – probably because their parents set unworthy examples - if we assume Confucius was correct - and it's certainly true that these Baby Boomer parents actually encouraged their children to rebel, as though willy-nilly rebellion is some sort of virtue. That is an enduring aspect of American culture, which remains undeniable today. Furthermore, Generation X was invariably instructed – at home and in the general culture – to not honor any of the gods of their allegedly totally-square "Greatest Generation" grandparents, whose rigid unhipness apparently proved that they were wrong in all ways and at all times. The result of Generation X is clear – being told they have no ancestors to honor, they honored only themselves.

That may sum up the expected view from China. What should be becoming clear is that grafting identical societal trends and beliefs from the West onto another part of the world is rather stupid. Of course, this is what the post-USSR claim of "universal values" necessarily implies, despite the fact that this chapter is clearly talking as much about the West as it is about China.

However, political revolutions and the waning of revolutionary spirit may take different forms, but they are both universal phenomenons. Let's return to the West's Generation X, which were the children of a political revolution, which clearly did not reach their aims for the majority of people.

What Generation X is most defined by, however, is alienation: they were encouraged to be attached to nothing and they abandoned political efforts to improve the world, probably because their parents totally failed in this regard. For whatever reason, the Baby Boomer generation could not provide counsel on what not to do - which, as every good craftsman knows, is just as important as knowing *what to do* - or they simply encouraged their children to be political fatalistic and uninvolved. The result was clear: Generation X rejected all authority – and thus the barest unity – and live today in consumerist individualism with at least three TVs in every house. They are the first generation to be weaned on "identity politics", which is the idea that *my* personal characteristics, background, ideas and needs matter the most; they pride themselves on "being above political parties" and are proud to be inconsistently all over the map. For them, earthly paradise will occur when *only their* ideas are followed, and I imagine that in their heaven it is just them all alone with God? Perhaps, like Sartre they feel that "hell is other people", as they are so very alienated.

Iranians do not try to separate politics and religion, but so does Generation X - just as they refuse to submit to a political doctrine they have rejected religious doctrines. This is why their religion is sensual, emotional and not logical; it is certainly a personalised "spirituality", which comes and goes as a muse might. Most aggravating to those who reject identity politics and search for bases of solidarity, their commandments are personalised and thus unknowable. This is why they are so much more easily offended than their parents or grandparents: their moral (and thus political) structures are totally unpredictable and undependable. They cannot even express their religious convictions when pressed. However, it is generally considered impolite to ask an American about religion, and the only people who bring it up in public are in America's lower class.

So we see how thoroughly the Western Baby Boomers' political failure has been passed on to their next generation: Even though Generation X is about to take the reins and have staffed the lower levels of government for decades, they cannot muster even a handful of prominent, successful politicians worthy of global admiration – everybody sees right through them and finds nothing but will-to-power and individualism. Thus there are nearly NO Generation X leaders in the West. Even France's Emmanuel Macron, born 1977, could almost be classified as a Millennial, and I note that his presidential portrait included not one but two smartphones - a true Generation X'er would have preferred a retro-nostalgic rotary phone with no working insides.

I'm not going to get into 3rd-generation Western Millennials other than – I see a lot of good things. They are certainly far less ego-driven (I'm a tough guy / I'm Wonder Woman) than the World War II generation, and a lot more community-minded than the Boomer generation. However, I note that if Western-style-TV-from-birth destroyed Generation X, it's possible smartphones-from-birth will do the same for Millennials. What is clear is that this generation has not just been weaned on identity politics but was their daily sustenance throughout childhood and adolescence; they will have to endure major personal dissonance when they realise that solidarity and not personal identity is the key to successful politics. It is quite easy and lazy to say that the idea that identity politics is "the answer", as Millennials have been led to believe, makes socialist-inspired politics impossible for them, but...it's still early. To paraphrase something often attributed to Che: A revolutionary can get tired, but then he ceased to be a revolutionary.

Now that we have charted the past of the West post 1960s, what about China? Are they really the exact same, just because they may watch the occasional Western movie when relaxing?

We must begin with an idea, which is undeniable, even if the West never can admit it: China's equivalent to the Baby Boomer generation certainly did NOT fail. Their Cultural Revolution was not just "tune in, turn on and drop out". Whether you condemn it or condone it, their student radicals *actually were given* tremendous political power (by a far more enlightened and politically-modern elder leadership) and thus actually DID change things. Indeed, a good proof of the Cultural Revolution's success is all the opprobrium heaped on it by the West today, where the reactionaries clearly won immediately: Nixon & De Gaulle re-elected, societal changes limited to culture and not political structure, etc.

It is interesting to read current reports from Egypt, seven years after Tahrir Square (where I reported during the fall of Mubarak): Egypt's revolution has also totally failed, and they are now following the same pattern as the West. Egyptians report that their failed revolution did at least produce more societal openness (mainly regarding sexuality), and allow more challenging of traditional and religious structures and ideas, but there is certainly less freedom, both economic and political. It's very titillating, for some, to talk about sexuality and atheism in public, but the West proves that these are very small and rather useless "freedoms". Such "freedoms" do not touch the core problems of the massive lower classes, nor do they prevent imperialism, stop wars or provide food and shelter. As Martin Luther King said: There is no freedom without economic freedom - and he was not talking about the 1%'s rights under neoliberalism.

Field Marshal-cum-president Abdel Fattah El-Sisi, tapped by the West to be their puppet once the democratically elected Mohamed Morsi was ousted in a 1%-led counter-revolution (Morsi's sin was that he was a Muslim democrat, and the West believes that is an oxymoron), now has the country pointed in a 100% neoliberal direction. His economic plan is typically neoliberal: providing only enough government services to prevent mass homelessness and starvation, in a rejection of the socialist idea that government must provide far, far more than that. We can predict that life for the average Egyptian will be far less free in the coming years because they will be far more poor, even if they have been "enriched' by the ability to discuss sex in public and the far less-desired right to be a proselytising atheist. Of course, there is no reason why Egypt's 1% would not make these cultural concessions in order to not touch the political and economic structure. Sadly, fake-leftists have won out in Egypt just as in the West - that's a major reversal from the incredible, short, powerful, almost indecipherable cry which swept Tahrir Square when news came that dictator Hosni Mubarak was stepping down. Certainly the celebrations that followed expected far more than just an El-Sisi.

So, Westerners can project their own experiences onto China as hard as they can, but the success of the Cultural Revolution is clearly unique, and it also obviously created a major postwar divergence for China, and one which is as unappreciated today as the Cultural Revolution itself. What we can do, and only perhaps, is to set our our gauge back, due to the Cultural Revolution's success: their "Greatest Generation", the one who actually won a war, is thus equivalent to the Western Baby Boomers. Why not, this exercise allows us to understand both China and the West a bit more?

Were I Chinese, that would make me a part of the "Baby Boomer" generation (I am 40); if I marry a Chinese lady quite soon and have children (Inshallah), then our kids would be in China's Generation X. But... is there such a generation already?

Bad news to report: Young Chinese say they aren't communist

I have Chinese friends, colleagues, and multiple family members who have lived for years in China. The Chinese of this generation – my peers – routinely, but not universally, say that yes, China is *not* communist.

Surprised I'd admit that, eh? Think I'm unobjective, do you?

This is truly a real issue, which must be examined. Is it possible that the Western press is actually right?

No, it is not.

These Chinese people I am discussing are all necessarily hugely influenced by the West. Even the native Chinese in my family emigrated away from China, even if they went back, and as an immigrant myself I can say: you don't become an immigrant be being 100% in love with your home country... or you would still be there. It's also very easy to have an inferiority complex about your home country, because the reality is that immigrants are literally trying to survive in a foreign land and make some friends: it certainly does not make one popular to move to a new country and proclaim: "My home is better than this." That is only for imperialists, who are there to steal and run, and thus are not true "immigrants"... and also for hard-headed, annoying journalists like myself!

My point here is – one should be wary of Chinese immigrants who claim that China is "not socialist" because immigrants are not accurate representatives of their home nations: the "Irish" of America are not at all like the Irish in Ireland. Immigrants are certainly a minority compared with the home population in the vast majority of national cases. Therefore, you should largely ignore that combative section headline three paragraphs above.

However, is there a genuine risk inside China? The two post-Cultural Revolution generations – do they believe their parents are the "Greatest

Generation" for winning their war?

I'm not sure about what's going on at the Chinese dinner table, but I know it matters

The Cultural Revolution veterans – who know from hard fighting and major personal sacrifice that capitalism is the enemy, and also that a bit of capitalism don't spoil no socialist show, who will never let capitalism dominate – have proven their totally-square socialist bonafides daily for decades. But the young "Boomer Generation" which runs from roughly 30-50 years old... many of them have only lived during the Deng-era capitalist reforms – are they solid socialists? And this group's children, China's "Millennials", might they be saying: "My father he ain't no Che Guevara – he's a total capitalist!"

The reality is that one's character is formed at the dinner table, when you are at the elbows of your elders.

"Is old Yeye (father's father) still going on about his time in the sticks during the '60s? Doesn't he know that my

Baba said *The Economist* called that a huge mistake? I sure don't want to go to the country – it smells like cow dung! Can I leave the table? I want to watch my favourite TV show again in my room."

If such a scene is happening regularly in Chinese homes...they will have a problem. That scene has been happening all over the West since the first Boomers started having kids in 1965, and it can happen to China. (The primary fault here is calling something your grandfather did "stupid" within earshot of your parents. Certainly that was a hanging offence in my household...)

The point here is, and it is more universal and theoretical than limited to China, is that such a problem is cultural, and one of corruption: not just monetary or judicial or political, but corruption at the dinner table night after night. This is social and thus ethical corruption. This is a common theme in Iranian politics, but something that the West almost refuses to even consider, which I find so very, very strange. Such concerns have been falsely labeled as "conservatism" by the West's fake-leftists. They fail to see that the dinner table is also where leftist revolutionaries can be formed... or not formed. Debunking the endless amount of capitalist propaganda takes more than just one discussion, and more than just one day of shouting slogans at a protest.

Dinner-table dynamics are the most complex part of any society, and they go beyond my Chinese ken. That's why I'm glad to see the answer so emphatically given in the title of Brown's book - *China is Communist, Dammit!*

The reality is that we non-Chinese simply must defer to new scholars like Brown on the question of whether China's two younger post-Cultural Revolution generations are committed communists or not. Cultures change, and quickly: I'm sure an alien visiting Iran in 1978 and 2018 – just 40 years – would be quite surprised at the changes (and pleasantly). Fairbank could never answer this issue, as he passed in 1991. Read Fairbank if you like, but you simply cannot expect answers about what Chinese 2018 culture is like.

However, what neither Fairbank, nor myself, nor you the reader have to completely defer to Brown is regarding the question of whether or not China is socialist. That is a question of the political analysis of China's structures, motivations and results. The idea that "all governments are the same", or some such nonsense, is mere political nihilism: socialism and capitalism have clear structures, policies and easily-traceable patterns which mostly contradict each other. Of course, what good is a law, which is ignored? The proof of socialism is "in the pudding" - the guarantee of China's *future* socialism... that is a question only those embedded in China can properly answer.

So why should I kowtow to the political analysis of China of a fictitious Chinese immigrant *if he or she lacks* broad political knowledge, or is overly-influenced by Western media? Indeed, to read Western journalism on socialism is to read (not even propaganda, because that requires intelligence) nonsense, stereotyping and sensationalism. "*I am Chinese, therefore my political analysis of China is superior to yours*" does not hold water. What does hold water is: "I am Chinese, therefore my *cultural* analysis of China is superior to yours."

Certainly. But it is quite easy to understand a lot of culture but zero politics, I think we'll all agree.

However, Brown is not just culturally literate regarding modern China but also obviously politically literate across multiple lands to an extremely high degree. I am not trying to sell his book: I am pointing out the validity of his analysis for our era. There are other such analysts as Brown, but painfully few, and they are essentially blacklisted from mass audiences. Western socialists simply do not live in an ideal situation regarding the availability of new, current, proper Chinese scholarship: Therefore, if Brown says China is communist (dammit!) in 2017, then we truly cannot find too many more trustworthy sources in English. Fairbank's book is two decades old and, despite all its mainstream marketing and its Harvard imprimatur, it is truly out of date in modern cultural analysis by a generation.

So you can ask your Chinese friends, as I do, and maybe they'll say that China isn't communist... and I wouldn't say that Brown "knows more about China" than they do – certainly – but I certainly feel quite comfortable positing that Brown may understand Chinese politics & geopolitics better than they do.

So is Chapter 8's headline a major concern in 2018 China, or not? Well...alienation, rampant individualism, and *corruption* of all types always are, aren't they?

'Generation X' is always an existential threat, and thus every generation must be righteous

Alienation was not discovered in a buried chest in 1946 in Europe – total dissatisfaction with one's culture and leaders, total disbelief in the power of religion, total post-traumatic stress disorder caused by war and pillage, total disbelief in the ability of humans to create a better world, and a feeling of certainty regarding the total power of human destructiveness is not at all a new sentiment in human history.

But alienation – while real and important and which cannot be ignored –

is something which faithful people don't have time for: they have to get to work.

However, alienation amid peace and plenty is indeed a problem limited to the first-world problem. And that is where China nearly is – the first-world.

They are not the first socialist country to get there – there is absolutely no doubt that the USSR was on par with the West economically and superior culturally – but they are the first one to reach their level *since the demise* of the USSR.

This means they are about to have first-world problems, like the Japanese tourists who get hospitalised by "Paris shock" - the disparity between the romantic image of Paris and the reality that most looks and treatment here equate to, when compared with polite Japan: "eat dirt and die". The medicine for such "victims" is clearly a strong dose of Chinese Cultural Revolution farm work, with a heavy emphasis on manure spreading... Absurdities aside, China truly represents the undeniable, at least medium-term, rebirth of socialism and communism *even though* the West declared it to be dead, and went whole-hog into the maximum form of capitalism possible, neoliberalism.

Because it is clearly not dead, their only choice is to co-opt it by falsely claiming its success. I imagine this is the root of Brown's title. Thus the cultural threat of denying China's "communist-ness" – and thus denying Chinese history and the Chinese experience today – is why President Xi is so important: a Gorbachev-like pandering to the West, or a Brezhnev-like tolerance of stagnation / corruption / black market / "reactionary dissent and sedition is what 'free speech' is"...is all that can turn the tide of China's rise.

However, it is obviously totally incorrect to reduce nations to just one person. Especially in socialist-inspired countries which had modern revolutions, focusing on the leader is a structurally inaccurate to describe their societies, which is why propaganda efforts do exactly this. China – like Cuba, Iran, etc. - is not run by a person but by a vanguard party which has grassroots-elected, democratic support. The preferred presidential candidates of Iran's current Supreme Leader Ali Khamenei have repeatedly lost, for example – these are modern pluralists democracies, not fiefs run by Macronian liberal warlords. Therefore, let us think of Xi only as a symbol for what all of China's middle-aged and elders should be like, both now and in the years to come:

The role of Xi: not spiking the ball on the 1-yard line

If Xi is part of China's "Greatest Generation", surely he rejects such a moniker: apart from being vain, it implies that China has already peaked - what sort of a leader does not want to see those in his charge surpass him in greatness? China has further to go, and many to help bring along with them, lest they be selfish capitalists.

The good news is: Xi spent 7 lice-filled years helping to bring the countryside up to modern levels during the Cultural Revolution – he will not be hospitalised by a rude French waiter.

And thus Xi is doing the opposite of Gorbachev – he is following in Mao's footsteps by leading anti-corruption campaigns, cleaning up corruption in the Peoples' Liberation Army and reducing propaganda contamination points the West so desperately needs open, now that they have no "hard power" options.

This is probably why Xi is so popular: he is doing what the People and the Party want – strengthening them and their chosen institutions. China has just ended their 2-term limit for presidents, with widespread domestic support, and I say: "Good call." Of course China should want their "Greatest Generation" (the Cultural Revolution generation) to stay in power: have you seen how bad the West's two ensuing generations are doing?! China is so close to being a humanity-improving superpower…and you want them to spike the ball on the 1-yard line because George Washington said so?

George Washington, the root cause of of the two-term trend, quit after two terms – it's pretty easy to hand the reins to your successor and say: "Keep stealing land and enslaving people: boom, economic growth issue – solved! Now don't bother me – I'm retired and have many slaves to beat and rape."

Xi is likely looking at Germany's liberal warlord-ette Angela Merkel – now in her 4th term of control – and seeing the positive national effects of long-term leadership within a democracy. He is likely also looking towards Iran's model, where the elected role of the Supreme Leader provides a constant counterweight in favor of ideological purity, against backsliding and in favor of the defense of Iran's popular, anti-imperialist, socialist-inspired revolution.

It's not all the economy, stupid – who is keeping track of the intangible and spiritual *within the* political? It is ironic that Communist China cares more openly for the issue of spirit than the rabidly secular West, as is abundantly proved by Brown's chapter *"21st Century Street Art for the Communist Body And Soul"*. This chapter actually proves to be the one a reader can return to time and again, as it documents state propaganda efforts (the good type) on totalitarian obsessions such as "Dedication", "Equality", "Freedom", "Harmony", "Honesty", etc. No such propaganda efforts exist in the West, because a government is what it promotes: the West promotes neoliberalism – no government – and so they produce no art or advertising designed to help people better themselves. The Western ideal of government is one which is supposed to not care nor get involved, and certainly not in ideas of spirituality or morality.

Germany's democracy is West European (bourgeois), Iran's is Islamic, and China's is Chinese socialist and none are perfect – as only God is – but we cannot deny that all three are indeed working democracies, with voting citizens, regular protests, repeated polls of support for their systems, etc. They have structural weak points, but they knew the weak points when they created and kept supporting their chosen system, although it seems totally incorrect to call postwar Germany's imposed system "chosen", and additionally there is the matter of the ongoing US occupation. At the very least, all three of these nations are certainly not authoritarian dictatorships nor neocolonial puppets, like most of the developing world is, and that is no small success to a journalist surveying the world in 2018. It's an absurdity that Iran and China are portrayed as such.

Xi is also looking at Russia, where Putin had the cunning to defy George Washington via recourse to legalistic explanations. This was not very honest, but the Russian people voted their approval repeatedly and the Russian system is just as democratic as any of the above three, so outsiders cannot say the Russian People don't largely have what they want within their system. No "humanitarian intervention" needed here either, please.

Because of the US and EU's military impregnability and the lack of any outside neo-colonial influence, they simply cannot comprehend the feeling among Iran, Cuba or others of being forced to operate under the gun. But certainly, in a time of crisis – WWII – the US abandoned the George Washington precedent to save their nation, as Roosevelt served 4 terms. Amid constant US belligerence Xi can fairly claim to be under threat. Fairly…but perhaps not after just one more decade of socialist economic success, especially as the Eurozone's never-reported "Lost Decade" is likely to turn into a Japanese-like Lost Score (The Eurozone's average annual growth rate from 2008 to 2017 was 0.6%. Japan 1991-2000: 1.4%. Japan 2001-2010: 0.7%.) France's Hollande or Macron cannot make the same claim legitimately, but they certainly did whatever they wanted via citing the threat of "Islamic terrorism".

So if China was communist, dammit, when Brown's book was published in 2017, they will certainly remain communist for another 5 or 10 more years under Xi. Rules are made to be broken, but not the dream of socialism.

Ramin Mazaheri

Conclusion: The world needs to learn from China's success since 1949

*I*t is said that one's true character is revealed after one becomes successful and achieves their dreams.

For some, like China, the dream is a moderately prosperous society for all. For some, like Iranians, the dream is paradise on earth as much as possible in order to earn paradise in the Afterlife.

For some, like the French, the dream is (I am quoting French people here) to be Gerard Depardieu: to be constantly eating, constantly drinking, constantly posing like an actor, to be considered a great artist just for posing, constantly arguing, constantly undermining everyone else's faith in anything, constantly believing that "contemptuous and skeptical" is a good baseline for a personality and starting point for social interactions.

For some, like Americans, the dream is everything in the world you can possibly imagine.

It's possible there may be some stereotypical nonsense here...

Let's stop with the nonsense: China is socialist, has succeeded, and needs to be emulated.

Capitalism is only a tool – in order to build wealth in order to have *something* to share – and a necessary one to construct communism, per Marx. China's ideals are certainly communist and there certainly is a very real, very effective, very concerned Communist Party in charge.

Anyway, communism is an ideal communists pray to (the atheistic communists, that is, who are definitely a tiny minority); socialism is what working people do to improve the world a bit more today.

Ultimately, this book asked the

question: What is "21st century socialism" when successful?

Because they are no longer susceptible to intense outside pressure, China is certainly the one which will most elucidate this answer, and with the most intense global and historical ramifications.

There is an easy way for China to put this very long-running "are they or aren't they communist" question to rest: give more support for other nations in regions which are certain to encounter Western resistance, and possibly hurt China's bottom line by doing so. Cuba used to do this, Iran does this...but these are costly. China helps far more than they get credit for, and certainly they gave in Korea and Vietnam, but their twin socialist successes in both economic growth and economic equality are getting to the point where cost is not truly a major issue *if they have socialist-inspired ideals*. China has remained rather (pre-WWII) Stalinist in foreign policy since Deng, and that can't continue forever. They aren't about to start giving major support to Palestine, sadly, but China needs to start throwing its weight around in favor of socialism again.

Foreign help will show the young generation that sacrifices must be made (thus showing them the urgent need to be content with "moderate prosperity"), and it will also force Westerners to accept their socialism-ness. All this increased acceptance of Chinese democratic socialism will only safeguard China further.

But if there's one thing China has done better than any socialist-inspired nation it's playing the long game. And the communist long-game is, clearly, nationalist Stalinism until universal Trotskyism. At least, that's what they will call it if communism goes universal (of course, some Trotskyists won't be happy until communism AND atheism goes universal, which is both sad, undemocratic and impossible).

However, the idea of Stalinism (socialism in one country), which Maoism has clearly incorporated, is essentially: take care of your own backyard, and wait for the rest of the neighbourhood to catch up. But what does China do when their backyard can't be made more beautiful? Either you harmoniously share the wealth with your neighbours, or the cycle of success ends and you wane into unharmonious capitalism. Incessant self-regard is certainly a form of corruption.

The needs of China, as it is the only socialist superpower left, need to start coming second behind needier socialist countries, and Iran is just one of them. How can China make Iran the hub of their "One Belt, One Road" or "New Silk Road" project and also allow it to be subverted and attacked by Western capitalists? When is the mutual defense treaty going to be signed? Iran is the only nation which defends the Islamic World west of India - how long can Iran keep doing it without major Chinese support? Socialism is sharing for mutual benefit, and not just within your own tribe: to quote the *I Ching*, from Chapter 13 "Seeking Harmony" – "*Seeking harmony within a clan, it is selfish and stingy*". China needs to move beyond its racial borders and countries like Korea and Vietnam - such an alliance with Iran would also further prove China's socialist bonafides.

I am not worried - such an open alliance is coming, and in my lifetime,

Inshallah. Both nations are governed by socialist-inspired democracies and vanguard parties, and both with the full backing of their People - they cannot lose.

Postscript:

Even though I consider Jeff J. Brown a friend and a colleague, I'd like to say that I wrote this book entirely without any personal involvement from him whatsoever. There can be no question regarding my objectivity. It is really quite simple: Fairbank's book needed denouncing, and Brown's book finally provided an excellent foil.

I hope this "double-book review" has shown just how different China scholarship can be, and also how much scholarship can change in just 20 years. I also tried to provide a few original ideas to put up for discussion, and to show how China's experience can be useful in other countries.

Finally: I'd like to point out that this series has been very clearly a political analysis of China, and not a cultural analysis. I have almost exclusively re-examined historical events and described political structures & policies. Brown and Fairbank are non-Chinese scholars who are qualified to make cultural analyses of China. However, political analyses are the privilege of every citizen – from the bus driver to the professor. Political analyses must be so very democratically available in order to constantly find – via merit and consensus – socio-political solutions to socio-political problems, the most pressing of which are, I believe, universal.

New analyses are needed on China, and on many other socialist-inspired nations – the events of 1989-91 were a long time ago, and the Great Recession is proving, still, that the alleged victory of capitalism was very short-lived. Whatever socialism's failures have been and are, the 1%-led Western model clearly cannot lead any country, as their leaders do not even wish to capably lead their own nations and communities – just their own fortunes.

Ramin Mazaheri

Article
NY Times: Are Little China Girls Ever Gonna Fall for Modern Love?

I was flying from New York to Silicon Valley on the "Job Creators' Red Eye", and I had a chance to catch up on some foreign cultural news from our nation's paper of record, *The New York Times.*

There was a very interesting item about the extremely backward practices of Asians regarding romance. This partly-ironic, mostly-pitying article focused on China.

Immediately, my blood ran cold. It had been running hot, as I was just reading the *Times*' recap of the misdeeds of Putin towards my millionaire friends running the Democratic party (pages 1-19 of their Section A). But when the page turned to his eastern ally I got as chilly as a crafty Chinese capitalist, which they all are. (How else could we possibly explain that growth rate?)

The reality is that romance is political: I, for example, date identities and not actual people. If you identify with Trump or (American God forbid) Putin, there is no romantic future for us. It's really quite logical – how can I date someone I refuse to even have a conversation with?

As a romantic, I accept reality. For example: Yes, there are 1 or 2 remnants of communism in China, but capitalism is a culture and not just an economic policy. It's not enough for us to have McDonald's all over China; what good is a Big Mac if the Chinese don't know why they have to incessantly eat them? Where's the continuous profit growth?

That's why articles like these are crucial, because we have to get the Chinese to not just eat like Americans, but to view romance like us too.

The best way to produce cultural changes – since there are no targets for our many bullets – is mocking and shame. *The New York Times* now publishes in Chinese, thankfully, and I hope our withering contempt translates well.

Just as we must attack their political leaders, their romance advice columnists must come under an attack no less serious! Both are extremely backwards and ignorant, obviously – just look at one of their leading romantic lights, Yang Bingyang:

"A former model, author of nine books and, she says, one of the first Chinese admitted to Mensa..."

Yes, that is the correct Western order: the fact that she is a model is her most impressive characteristic. I was surprised there was not a link to any of her pictures because it has been nearly 11 minutes since I saw a woman nearly naked – what is this, Saudi Arabia?

"Our world has been hijacked by political correctness," Ms. Yang said. *"I'm criticized for telling the truth about the differences between men and women."*

The best journalism hangs them with their own words! Political Correctness has only liberated us in every way; there are no differences between men and women. When are we going to start using NSA spy capabilities for apprehending anti-PC terrorists who make such offensive declarations in their own homes? I'm sure Hillary would have implemented this already!

She elaborated: *"A man's M.V. (mate value) is determined by his age, height, looks, wealth, I.Q., emotional quotient, sexual capacity and willingness to make a long-term commitment... The eight elements in a woman's M.V. are her 'age, looks, height, bra cup size, weight, academic degrees, personality and family background'."*

Frankly, this is abhorrent – I would imagine this will one day be included in our justifications to the UN for a humanitarian intervention in China.

Not only do I not notice colour, ethnicity or shape, but I am far, far above being concerned about a woman's age. Surprisingly, this created a problem for me when I tried to take that 13-year old Thai girl out of the country. "I don't see superficialities like age or looks, you bigoted Trumpers," I screamed at the Thai border police!

But I guess the Chinese really are White in a way – there's "bra size" instead of "hip size". Still, I can't have anything truly in common with such a sexist society.

And I thought they had a fetish for tiny feet? It seems they don't talk about that enough, but I hope they bring back that practice soon – but only during work hours in my Chinese factories, of course.

"Don't have sex for the first few months," Ms. Yang tells women.

I immediately fell out of my first-class seat laughing at this. In fact, I had to go back to the coach section and tell my work "teammate" Fazlollah, even though I can't stand him. We all call him "Lefty" because no one can pronounce his name.

"How long do men have to wait to have sex in your country," I asked Lefty.

Fazlollah straightened up, leaned forward in his seat to not bother the woman in the aisle seat next to him and worriedly whispered, "Is this really the place for such a conversation?"

Those uptight Asianers... so repressed. I hope many of our soldiers are liberating their women around our many army bases in the region.

Fazlollah tried to change the subject to Putin's evilness, but there are some things which are even more important, so I loudly insisted he tell me how long I have to wait for sex when I visit his native country.

"Well, boss, I'm certainly not going to tell you about me and my wife, but I'll say that most of my friends waited one year before having sex with their fiancees or wives."

I burst out laughing again!

Lefty added: "But I have a younger friend, and he says the newer generation has no patience and can only wait for 6 months."

My God, Fazlollah's people really are a bunch of animals. The way they treat their women is just beyond insulting, because we all know women are as desirous of immediate sex as men are. So, really, their women are animals too. But the sheer waste of resources – taking her out, buying her food, spending your time –

and then not getting anything out of it?!

I went back to my paper, where the Times interviewed a different romantic columnist, named simply Ayawawa.

"Many of Ayawawa's fans consider her the personification of the success they crave for themselves: attractive, married to a man she describes as a loving husband, the mother of two children."

Again, attractiveness is what is most important for Chinese women – good, they are learning about Western feminism. But given the rest of those unusual craved-for successes, they clearly still have much to learn.

"Chinese schools don't offer a proper education in love and relationships," Mr. Lu, a male romantic advice columnist, said in another interview. *"People get their ideas mostly from TV dramas."*

I never heard of any American getting their ideas from TV. We're a free-thinking people, after all. The Asians are just so inscrutable... that's why we have given up scrutinizing them for any cultural coherence and are just going to turn them into Americans.

True, I was taught about sex in school

when I was 12 – we took that as a sign that our community wanted us all to start having sex. There's no stigma attached to 13-year old pregnancies anymore – it's just the sign of a good student who pays proper attention. But we never did get any sort of real education about relationships – those are personal subjects never to be discussed, like God and my tax returns!

"For women, spending more time with a man deepens her love. But for a man, the longer he stays with a woman, the less he loves her," Mr. Lu posted this month.

That's funny: I told the same thing to my 3rd wife. She got very upset, and that's when I remembered the David Bowie song, *"China Girl"*. The chorus to *"China Girl"* goes: *"And when I get I excited, my little China girl, says 'Oh baby, just you shut your mouth.'"*

Cheekily, I told that last part to her.

When I woke up in the hospital I asked the doctor if I had been hit in the head with a frying pan. He said I was hit by the phone my wife uses to have our dinner delivered. I really was asking for it: I knew we didn't need a landline anymore.

During my recuperation and divorce

trial I had time to listen to that whole Bowie album, and I see that I was wrong to quote him in the first place.

The chorus to another song, "*Modern Love*", is "*Never gonna fall for modern love*". I don't know why I ever took advice from some impractical romantic musician...

Like I told my 4th wife just before we signed our pre-nup: Love is really all about material benefits. Luckily, *The New York Times* never, ever takes their eye off that ball.

"*Both of them advise women to manipulate men to gain material benefits,*" said Ms. Lu, a founder of an online feminist journal in China. Now take it easy – she's just a Western-style feminist and not a communist, because she didn't dare criticise manipulating people to gain material benefits, which is basically the definition of capitalism.

"*The question is, Why in China is it women who scheme to get men to commit to marriage? Why, when it comes to marriage, are women the sellers and men the buyers? It's because women don't have the space to develop themselves.*"

See, this is what modern love is: Romance is a transaction! It should be ruled by the laws of the market, not the laws of nature or even morality. You don't have to be a feminist to get that! And we're going to make sure the Chinese understand this.

Let's give women the chance to be the buyers, finally, eh? That's equality.

Let's have men be the ones who scheme to get women to commit to marriage, eh? That's social and moral progress.

"It's sad to see, when the economy has produced so many more opportunities, that more and more women believe that getting married is superior to working hard and achieving a successful career," she said.

I want to hire this person to run one of my factories in Shenzhen! Yes, of course nothing is more important than working hard in one of my factories! Certainly not your family life!

If I had more workers like her I think I could shave nearly 7 cents off the price of my electronics? But we in New York City can't do anything with Chinese women who cling to outdated desires and notions.

"Liang, for example, is trying to lose weight and improve her makeup skills and is practicing baking."

Sophisticated reader that I am, I realise that this poor Liang is meant to be portrayed as a sad, pathetic loser... even though at 29 she has a fiancé, office job and is apparently not fat.

But she's a loser – and all modern women who read *The New York Times* will agree with me – because by selfishly putting her future family first she's setting back a woman's right to devote her body and soul to work for me.

The article concludes with this appallingly out-of-date and unfocused woman's pathetic view:

"The differences between men and women are inborn. I take these ideas seriously because I want a better life for myself, not because I'm eager to make the world better for women."

There is a word for this type of woman: a misogynist. This Chinese woman, because she wants romantic love, a family, and a home life which includes the smell of fresh baked fortune cookies, is actually a woman-hating, repressive, backwards misogynist.

And she's obviously some sort of Putin supporter – or at least Trump – because she doesn't realize that identity politics requires her to divide the world into women versus men. By not trying to make the world better for only women, she is fighting for the wrong side!

How are we going to divide China if we can't foist identity politics on them?

And the baking, my God, the baking!!!! For a modern woman she may as well be an African-American person asked to pick cotton!

Frankly I don't know why her fiancé even wants her? She's clearly going to be a drag on his bottom line: baking can be done cheaper by others; that's less time spent earning wages; and the emotional ideas she's taking seriously are so detached from economics that there is no point to even discuss them.

But most appalling, again, is that there are inborn differences between men and women. It's just not true and you know it!

Both of them work just fine on my factory floor – they are basically interchangeable. I'm proud to report that when a man drops from exhaustion we replace him immediately with a woman with no drop off in my profitability.

Now that is modern, and I love it.

(Originally Published on June 23, 2017)

Ramin Mazaheri

Article
What does the Tao say about Europe and Islam?

Look - we are just butting heads here, we Muslims and Europeans. Constantly arguing over whose ideology and culture is superior.

And all the while the 1% of families who own the 99% of the world's wealth are just looking down and laughing at us as they read their stock tickers. And that 1% is multicultural, multiracial and practices multiple religions. They don't care about European or Muslim or whatever – they care about money: yours.

But for us 99% the clash of

civilizations is happening...or has happened, or will happen, or will not happen – who knows?

With such confusion reigning, let's do what two seemingly irreconcilable parties often do – turn to a mediator.

Our cultures have ceased helping, so let's turn to a totally different culture: I propose China.

Yes, China. They do have a UN veto, and they don't just give those away.

"China's a biased country – they have plenty of native Muslims," shouts Brussels. Indeed, 20+ million: more than Europe if you exclude Turkey.

"China's a biased country – they're scared if we take over they'll lose pork and alcohol," shouts Riyadh. Indeed, as well. China seems rather fond of those two.

No cultural mediator could be perfect. However, China is not a country.

China is a continent – it just never took credit for it like Europe did. It never even got a grudging "sub-continent" designation like India.

China has nearly 60 ethnic groups, 8 major linguistic groups and hundreds of dialects. This is after the societal unification brought about by Communism, so imagine what it used to be like?

They know all about Warring States periods and Three Kingdoms becoming many kingdoms, and too many Han here and not enough Turkic tribes there.

We know they know about building walls.

So I propose we let the Chinese mediate on the question of how Europe should treat its Muslim communities, and how Muslim communities in Europe should treat Europeans.

"Not fair, you are already thinking in a binary-and-interactive fashion like yin and yang theory, so you yourself are biased!"

Shut up Paris! Quit playing the devil's advocate for your own amusement!

Let the mediation begin!

Ahhhhh so... China discuss this long ago. You still here?! Heap great disgrace!

Therefore if a great country gives way to a smaller country,
It will conquer the smaller country.
And if a small country submits to a

great country,
It can conquer the great country
Therefore those who would conquer must yield
And those who conquer do so because they yield

(Rustling breezes, gurgling brook, someone playing a reed flute)

This is the 2nd part from Chapter 61 of the Tao Te Ching, written around 500 BC and still being misunderstood by hippies today.

In China's most humble opinion, this is the most relevant passage of the chapter to our discussion, so let's start there.

Being barely able to grasp the meaning of the Tao as humble China already is, China is going to assume a lot of this poem is already obvious to you. But you are paying China to mediate, so....

The "*great country*", here, is Europe.

They are economically advanced – *cough cough* imperialism *cough cough* – and their dominance cannot be denied.

And Europe is after all...located in Europe. It is, therefore, full of "Europeans".

That is really the main point – China really likes to examine the fundamentals, please to excuse us.

In each of the European countries you have a dominant group, with a long and impressive culture. In nearly all the countries the culture is not as long or impressive as China's, of course... but China has digressed foolishly here.

You also find a dominant religion (Christianity of some form) and a dominant ethnic class (Latin, Anglo Saxon, Celtic, Slavic, etc.)

Ahhhh, but did the immortal Tao counsel Lao Tzu to write: *"A great country says what's what, so shut the hell up about it"*?

Not at all, the Tao guided Lao Tzu to write: *Therefore if a great country gives way to a smaller country*

That very notion is a very different starting point from what China reads from the very un-Tao-ed European mass media, or their governments, or the drunk at the local bar when there are no Brown people around.

China suggests – please to try hard to follow – that *"great"* Europe *"gives way"* to the "*small country*".

The "*small country*" here... being all those minorities of Roma, Muslims, Africans, Coptic Egyptians, Black animists, Eritrean atheists, etc. within Europe.

China does not mean this in the opening of the gates to more refugees, necessarily - although Europe should - but China is focused on remedying the major lack of social harmony in Europe today.

China is advising the Great Country to give way *culturally*, to live in harmony with the Tao and thus each other.

China notes that the Great Country has many more natural advantages over these Small Countries – demographic advantages, national homogeneities, social advantages – that it should hardly be worried about losing its "national identity".

Conquering means the smaller "integrates" into the greater

And this has already proven to be a workable model.

China notes that in France there are many Blacks and Muslims who are 100%

proud to be "French", and rightfully so. France has much to admire. The great country let them in and assimilation was mastered by many: the smaller country was conquered.

Supreme good fortune – nothing was unfavorable.

The great country will always conquer eventually through the natural process of absorption. With any proper absorption – as with food – it eventually becomes part of the main organism.

You are what you eat. If you reject what you eat often enough...you must be sick. Maybe you have dysentery and will eventually die. It is serious. Please do not use China's chopsticks.

But this takes cultural digestion takes time and cannot be forced. Europe did not already conquer so many members of the Smaller Country by thinking it can eat foreigners whole and easily spit out whole Europeans.

If you ease back and watch the show and enjoy your Great Country feeling of fullness – all will be well in the end.

So what can we infer that the Tao Te Ching does not advise, in this cultural context?

The Great Country should not be aggressive at all – it should be satisfied and secure in its own dominance. A lack of aggression translates into tolerance, patience and generosity for the small.

China senses something is sticking in the craw of perhaps Europe's most difficult... yes London?

"All I'm reading is about 'Great Country' responsibilities – what about the responsibilities of the 'Small Country'?"

Why are you so impatient? Most unharmonious. But let's move on to lines 3 and 4

The cycle has waxed, and now the cycle wanes

And if a small country submits to a great country,
It can conquer the great country

Indeed, "submitting" is what China now advises for Europe's Muslims – the Small Country.

China knows there are some immigrants who move to a place and never learn the language or make new friends. They choose to remain isolated in their own immigrant communities and seemingly live exactly as they did before.

The plus side is – they seem perfectly content, are hard workers and commit no great crimes.

China knew a non-Muslim English journalist here (a journalist!) who lived in Paris for 15 years and said he could only order a baguette in the French language – his wife did all the talking for him. China reports that this guy is hilarious, was a big success and should not be stoned to death for his stubbornness or lack of language skills.

China must note – for those who don't actually know immigrants at all – the ones who don't submit are only a small part of the very first arrivals.

The reason is – usually all they do is work at some lousy job! They are tired. They are tired from working to pay for their kids' food and shelter; they are tired from cooking and cleaning. If they want to see their immigrant friends in their little spare time, or just watch TV, then give them a break!

"Old dogs can't learn new tricks," these people believe. Fine, let's move on from them.

China notes that the ones who do submit to the dominant culture are truly living and are immeasurably enriched.

China knows one goofy immigrant journalist in Paris very well - he works for Iran's PressTV. He can't imagine living in France without having adopted their language and customs, or not having befriended French people. China says this guy has replaced many of his ideas and habits for French ideas and habits, and he is better for it.

China notes that this guy already had plenty of room for improvement.

The 2nd generation – China must say here – always submits to the Great Country to a great extent. They have to – they go to the schools, where peers and teachers ensure it. They also grow up watching the local TV, movies, music, etc.

In Europe you now have 3rd generation and 4th generations of Muslims. In a few more generations – like the Normans in France – they'll be 90% "French" and only 10% other. Are the

Normans so bad? Are the Muslims as bad as invading Vikings?

Of course not. Exaggeration is an extreme, and so the Tao naturally now changes from irony to seriousness.

But even Vikings had principles

However, China warns that to force submission on matters of deepest principle is inherently against the way of the Tao. It is extreme.

If one submits or subverts their own morals simply to please the Great Country – such a person clearly is not operating with the Tao, yes? This a weak person, greatly at fault.

So Great Country Europe cannot force Muslims to take a drink if it violates their morals. They cannot force Muslim women to dress in a way they consider to be immodest – that would cause them to feel great shame quite unnecessarily.

The Great Country must yield when no one is hurt or when no laws broken. China does not advise writing new laws which they know the Smaller Country will break because it is against their morality!

This is needless antagonism, and cannot but turn out poorly.

And China notes that for the Small Country, Muslims, to conquer means acceptance by the Great Country.

The Small Country will conquer by gaining acceptance for some of their minority ways, which they feel it would be immoral to compromise.

If Muslims submit – integrate in a sincere fashion – then China is confident that they will convince the Great Country that the submission need not be total.

Such submission is slavery, something Europe renounced, yes?

China does not understand how Europe's feelings could even get hurt by simply seeing a hejab or a Brown person turning down alcohol.

China says: you are too sensitive. China believes that Europe's pride is hurt – they feel they have been colonized by the United States.

China cannot give any advice here... because China does not have this problem. Hahahahahahaaha!

And China will never have this problem... as the US will submit to us!

Hahahahahaahahahaha!

Who says the Chinese have no sense of humor?!

Yes, Europe's pride has been hurt because they are no longer the #1 colonizer – the student has surpassed the teacher. And when the pride of a Great Country is hurt it looks for a scapegoat – a Small Country – because it is not admitting self-blame, which would enable it to correct its internal position in way which is in accordance with the harmonious Tao.

China knows that if we ever hope to absorb the Small Country of the United States – so very small to us, so young, over-sensitive and amusing – we know what we have to do: Look to the Tao Te Ching and *give way to the smaller country*.

Otherwise, those ignorant capitalist savages will give us much indigestion! You think millions of Muslims are bad – imagine millions of Americans in Europe! Muslims aren't so bad now, eh?

But to properly absorb the smaller, if it is wise, China will return to lines 5 and 6:

Therefore those who would conquer

must yield

And those who conquer do so because they yield

So you see China already has a plan

Not just a mediation solution, but a plan.

A plan for taking over the US, and a plan for taking over Europe! But only via the extension of harmony.

China says to the Great and Small Countries of Europeans and Muslims: "Get your act together and seek mutual harmony or else we are coming implement it!"

This is why China advises all Europe to seek harmony immediately.

China would like to point out that our modern Communist Revolution won, and we gained plenty *because* we sought harmony. China is still growing and has made huge strides in decreasing inequality and increasing solidarity, while Europe is in total economic disarray, even after profiting from two centuries of imperialism in the Muslim world and four centuries of imperialism in the New World.

China reminds Europe to read a newspaper once in a while: the European Union and Eurozone is neo-imperially feeding upon its Smaller Nations, as it once did with China.

China notes that the Small Country Muslim communities are poor and receive very little of these neo-imperial spoils. They also certainly have no political power to organize these capitalist and counter-revolutionary machinations which clearly violate the Tao up the yin-yang.

China stresses: Communism is a truly modern ideology, much more modern than nationalism (although in Europe it is mostly imperialist "jingoism"), and it promotes ethnic unity 100%. You wouldn't have this crisis under communism, for certain, and the average European could concentrate on its real enemy – capitalism.

China notes: Join socialism and there is only a true, modern brotherhood between us...and China will not be forced to gently conquer you.

China feels the time for judgment has come in this mediation

Europe must first return to lines 5 and 6. They require meditation.

Therefore those who would conquer must yield
And those who conquer do so because they yield

Perhaps you should take a break? Maybe go outside and look at the moon? If it is daytime perhaps you can glance at the sun, noting its munificent magnificence shining down.

Have you done that? Is the meaning clearer?

Here is China's decision:

China is telling Europe: hey, if you want Muslims to fit in - stop harassing them. They are already here, and they are mostly in your underclass, so stop trying to take away their morality, too – their religion. That is going too far, so change. Be a bit more generous and humble!

China is telling Muslims: hey, stop

your crying or go home. You have to learn the new ways in the new country and change. If your old country is so great – you certainly have a valid passport, which allows you to return there. Be a bit more generous and humble!

China doesn't want to gloat but...

China has communism and the Tao! It's a good time to be Chinese.

And now we humbly now cites the following and final four lines of Chapter 61:

> *A great nation needs more people;*
> *A small country needs to serve.*
> *Each gets what it wants.*
> *It is fitting for a great nation to yield.*

(Rustling breezes, gurgling brook, young woman with an enormous hat pads by in sandals)

That's how it is!
These lines mean:
"Europe is great so it truly needs

more people. These people are coming from small, poor countries, and so they need to serve in order to improve their station. Each side will get what it wants...if Europe acts without fault and yields first, in acceptance."

China is now happy to serve you all an enormous fortune cookie we have baked for your honor and enjoyment! The huge fortune cookie was needed to fit the preceding paragraph, which is your fortune to meditate on.

Your lucky numbers are 6, 17, 22, 37 and 42.

The cookie is halal of course. Hahaha, just kidding – China is worldly enough to know that those rules don't apply here. Just making with the food and the fun – everyone likes that! China is now serving rice wine, but our Uighur delegation says they are high enough off God. Must be nice to be Uighur!

I would join the festivities but I've been given the honor to moderate – I want to do my best to promote harmony. Also I have much work to do: China needs more people, as we are a great nation.

Tao Te Ching - Chapter 61

A great country is like low land:
It is the meeting ground of the universe,
The mother of the universe.
The female overcomes the male with stillness,
Lying low in stillness
Therefore if a great country gives way to a smaller country,
It will conquer the smaller country.
And if a small country submits to a great country,
It can conquer the great country
Therefore those who would conquer must yield,
And those who conquer do so because they yield
A great nation needs more people;
A small country needs to serve.
Each gets what it wants.
It is fitting for a great nation to yield.

Originally Published on February 21, 2017

About Author

Ramin Mazaheri is the chief correspondent in Paris for PressTV. He was educated at the University of Missouri-Columbia and has lived in France since 2009. He has been a daily newspaper reporter in the US, and has reported from Iran, Cuba, Egypt, Tunisia, South Korea and elsewhere. He is also the author of *Socialism's Ignored Success Story: Iranian Islamic Socialism*. His work has appeared in various journals, magazines and websites, as well as on radio and television. He can be reached on Facebook.

Made in the USA
Middletown, DE
12 February 2021